GOD

IS

NOT DEAF

IBIKUNLE FAYEMI

Published by:
Ibikunle Fayemi
5, Tijani Bello Street, Ojodu-Ikeja, Lagos, South-West Nigeria
+2348127718107 and +2348033511207

Copyright © Ibikunle Fayemi 2017

ISBN: 978-978-958-819-0

Designed & Printed by:
Kolad Prints
41, Olorunsogo street,
Mushin, Lagos
South-West Nigeria
+2348063708988
+2348023599007

APPRECIATION

All I want to say to the people mentioned below is: thank you very much. You were my strength while I was weak. Your gift of love warmed my heart during my "coldest winter ever", during my era of trial and tribulation.

Omoba Leke Adesanya, Otunba Bolaji Osinuga, Omoyemi Adetoun Ojo, Adeniyi Fayemi, Adebimpe Sonuga, Femi Sonuga, Yatta Kamara, Bolajoko Fayemi Odejayi, Ayodele Fayemi, Shola Fayemi, Bayo Fayemi, Roselyne Abraham, Olatunde Fatinikun, Monisola Olofin- Fatinikun, Gbenga Olushina, Nicole Meyers, Oyekunbi Odelola-Adesanya, Tokunbo Anissi Awosusi-Oderinde, Erelú Túndé Fúnké Welsh, Bill Freeman, Omotayo Michael-Anubi, Dare Olofinjana, Yeside Ayannuga-Goss, Oluyemisi Onipede Cardoso, Adams Akintola, Omolara Lawal and Gbemisola Pedro, Mrs Sandra Rayford (May her soul rest in perfect peace)

I will also like to thank Mr Samuel Okoye for guiding me through facets of publishing this book. Not only did he assist in editing the book, he also added a fine polish to it.

Finally, I will like to thank Abimbola Adewole for providing me with the emotional anchor during this phase of my life. Not only was she the first to read the unrefined chapters of this book, she is also the one that added spices of love to my life.

DEDICATED TO

This book is dedicated to the memory of my father and mother, Mr Ayodele Fayemi and Mrs Olusola Sonuga-Fayemi. They solved some problems for me before I even recognized the problems. May their souls continue to rest in perfect peace.

TABLE OF CONTENTS

INTRODUCTION

When I was strategizing on what the title and contents of this book will be, I asked someone for her opinion. l said, "How about a title that says: "God is Not Deaf"? "And she answered, "We all know that." Meaning we all know that God is not deaf. Then I said, "So why do some people make so much noise when praying to God?" And she aptly responded, "Because a lot of people are deaf".

This book is to appeal to people not to be deaf anymore. If they listen, in stillness, to God within themselves, they will discover that God is not deaf. So, they should stop making all the noise they called prayer. The kingdom of God does not come with observation because it is already "within you." Even Jesus was reported to have said so many years ago. "God Is Not Deaf."

Time is said to be the father of all truth. And, knowledge is simply a means to an end, a useful tool to live a successful and a happy life. If your knowledge, your method works for you, fine. I am happy for the individual who has found what works for him or her. Mine, which I have been working on for the past twenty three years, works for me. It has provided me with contentment and inner joy. "...unlike knowledge, understanding cannot be taught. It must be achieved." — Dave Donovan

For me, this is the best of time for me to die. Because I have lived fully. Because I have lived satisfactorily. But until then, I continue to live, love, laugh. I continue to live a fulfilling life. "God" is not blind in my life. "God" is not deaf.

CHAPTER 1

GOD IS NOT DEAF

A lot of people in my part of the world do not know what God is. And, this ignorance shows in the unsatisfactory life they are living. As a mystic, I know it is possible to have a two-way communication with "God" without being schizophrenic. This two-way communication is what provides authentic spiritual guidance, and not the noise making one-way communication presently going on with the majority, even with the people you will think ought to know better.

In an attempt to communicate with "God", these people make so much noise. And consequently, they disturb the peace and tranquillity of other people. It is an ethical axiom that our rights stop where other people's rights begin. Yes, the noise-makers in the guise of worshipping "God" have a right of worship, but so do others have a right to their peace and tranquillity.

If I were them, I will heed the advice once given that they should go inside their rooms, where no one can neither see nor hear them, whenever they want to pray. I love to sleep. I love to sleep until my eyes open by themselves. This, again, is one of the simple pleasures of life that I thoroughly enjoy. You can call me blessed when it comes to achieving pleasant, deep, invigorating sleep.

But......

One morning in 2015, a loud noise woke me up around 6:30 am, Alas! It was a loudspeaker blaring the Christian prayer directly into my room. Well, so it seems. It was coming from close quarters though. It was so loud I could not concentrate on my own early morning meditation. I saw the Alfa living in the house opposite my own peeping down the street. He too wanted to know where his competitor's loud noise was coming from.

I went down and I saw two men holding loudspeakers as if holding machine guns. A lady without loud speaker was with them. They were in the "wa gba Jesu si inu aye e" mode. If the street was divided into two, where they were standing may conveniently be the middle. And that was where they were, attacking the neighbourhood with their "every knee shall bow, every tongue shall confess that Jesus is lord" imperial arrogance.

The missionary that laid the foundation had the colonizers' almighty guns backing them up. Their purported "saving souls" gentility actually was backed up with the overbearing power of the guns to colonize the souls of friends and foes alike.

But.....that was then, and this is now.

So, I walked up to these modern day evangelists who had robbed me of my early morning sweet sleep and my early morning meditation. "Guys, this is unfair to the whole community. Your loud noise is depriving us of our early morning sweet sleep. Other people have their own way of calling unto their Gods too. Please stop."

He looked at me as if I was the devil itself preventing him from spreading the word of his "God". And I looked at him as if he was the devil depriving me of enjoying my "God-given" gift of sleep to the fullest. The noise did stop. And I left them in peace. I had intended to seize their two loudspeakers if they had not stopped.

His freedom of speech does not extend to polluting the environment with loud noise. And his freedom of worship does not extend to disturbing my sleep. It is axiomatic that our rights stop where other people's rights begin.

Doing the right things the right way has no substitute. Failure to understand this is what led to our wobbling. "God" is not deaf. Also, as a mystic, I am aware of a "God" that can read minds, that can speak in a silent voice. A voice so silent it will be drowned in the cacophony of noise making some people mistake for prayer.

Stop all these ostentatious display of piety that was the hallmark of the Pharisees that were rebuked in antiquity. Go ahead, go on, start striving to do the right things the right way, and, maybe, just maybe "God" will speak to you. And, then, you will stop acting like the prophets of Baal in antiquity.

We are not making as much progress as the rest of the world. And that is not because we do not pray enough. We do have millions of people who continue to disturb the peace of their community with their fervent, ostentatious prayers.

We are not making that much progress because majority of us have become rigid in our thinking, and consequently, stagnant in our progress. We have lost the ability to interpret reality effectively.

No wonder our unending slide down the ladder of progress.

Why is the Naira so weak and the dollars and pounds so strong? Is it because we need more crusade and night vigil?

Cru...what? Sade? Night what? Vigil? If it is not so sad, it will be funny.

Can any smart person see ice and say it comes from inside fire? Can any smart person see love, peace and joy and say it comes from negativity? Can steady, positive progress be sustained without relevant knowledge, creativity and innovation?

I think accurate interpretation of reality is fundamental to all human progress. And clarity of mind, not prejudice, is needed to interpret reality effectively.

However, clarity of mind may elude any mind burning with anger, hatred, and greed.

So, take a greed test, if it is positive, come and enrol in my class. I will teach you how to survive on less, how to cut your coat according to your fabrics, how to consistently enjoy the simple pleasures of life.

"God" is not deaf. It is just that the prayers of those who do not follow the law, those who are not diligent in their duties, those who are corrupt, are abomination to "Him".

In addition, no one can substitute incompetence for "God".

Listen to the case of this young man. He does not have a good grasp of the English language. One can tell from his responses. But that can be excused. After all, English language is a second one to him, and not his mother's tongue. However, his arrogance is blinding him from recognizing that he has received a half-baked education.

He is not in good grasp of current reality. When he opens his mouth, he is describing a different reality apart from the one we shared in common. He continues to make the same mistake by thinking the way he thought before he finds himself in a stagnation mode.

He knows most things about "God". He thinks nothing is impossible for "God". And he thinks that prayer is the master key for all possibilities. But he is incompetent in his profession. Yet he thinks it is the "haters" that refuse to recognize the good work of his hands.

Now, he should answer this question quick: has the majority of Nigerians not been praying ceaselessly in the last two years for the betterment of this country? Can anyone produce the proof of what has truly improved since then?

When he makes money from corrupt practices, he tags it "God's blessing." And he proceeds to his preferred place of worship for thanksgiving, to give "God" His share of the dirty lucre.

He thinks the government is this or is that. But he could not see the correlation between his archaic thinking that produces nothing, his voracious appetite for imported goods, services, ideology, and the continuously declining Naira.

The day he recognizes that he is a part of the problem of this country, is the day the seed of this country's greatness will begin to germinate. God is not deaf.

PMB took over the mantle of power in 2015. And, as at March, 2017, He is presently on medical leave in London. And, I wish him well, not just for his own sake, but also for our sake.

Things are not well here in Nigeria. One dollar is now changing for over five hundred Naira. Yes, fuel scarcity is gone. But....

Back to PMB

I am convinced he is tackling corruption head on. He has nothing to lose. With the curbing of corruption, incompetence will flee, hopefully.

When people realize that corruption can no longer get them what they want, they will have no choice but to do, not just their best, but also what is necessary. Doing the right things the right way will then become the norm, and not an aberration.

With the mitigation of corruption, competence level will rise. Progress will begin in ernest. Sustainable development will come. And then, we will be able to take our seat in the circle of developed nation.

But...
For this to happen, PMB must continue to tackle corruption. He must curb it. This is how I see it. It is not just government officials that are corrupt, a lot of us are expert swimmers in the ocean of corruption.

Sometimes in 2009, armed robbers snatched my vehicle. The Police found it abandoned somewhere but without the key. The Police demanded 50,000 Naira bribe before I could retrieve my vehicle (Corruption). I called a "rewire" to help me out and he ruined the ignition (Incompetence). I called another "rewire" and he collected money to buy another ignition but ended up using the old one (Corruption). The armed robbers that started this whole ordeal were indiscipline. Instead of acquiring education/skills that required the kind of patience that was born out of discipline, they opted to extend their indiscipline into the territory of corruption.

The question that needed to be asked too is: was the source of income I used in purchasing the vehicle that was stolen untainted by corruption?

Hmmmm

We cannot have a national rebirth without individual rebirth. We must begin to give what we want to get. "God" is not deaf.

Just like everyone is entitled to her own opinion, so also is everyone entitled to his own delusion. However, opinions rooted in delusion may lead to wasted efforts. And wasted efforts always lead to disappointment, dejection. And if care is not taken, it may lead to depression.

Therefore, as everyone is entitled to her own opinion, so also is everyone entitled to his own challenges, his own suffering. For every right, there is a corresponding obligation. God is not deaf.

Life is tough. At least for most people it is tough. We ought to look for ways to make it easy for ourselves without making it tough for others.

We should not dig a hole to fill another hole. Neither should we rob Peter to pay Paul.

If, wherever we are, and whenever we leave, some people say, "life was easier when he/she was here," without making it tough for others, we should consider ourselves to be a good person, a good leader.

We can tell a good person, a good leader, by how he/she handles ethical issues. Ethical issues are always serious issues to the discerning minds. Without strong ethical standard, a country is enmeshed in decadence, unable to erect strong institutions.

Is this not why it was said that "righteousness exalts a nation"? God is not deaf.

At this phase of my life developmental issues that concern Nigeria are of utmost importance to me.

Of course issues that concern human development, happiness and success are intricately linked with issues of Nigeria in my mind.

If the individuals do not grow, if they are not successful and happy, how can this country progress? And those who are waiting for Nigeria to be good before things are good for them may have to wait for a very long time.

Some people have mastered "God" and all that is in heaven. I have not. But I have mastered how to live a fulfilling life, with more or with less, outside of Nigeria and in Nigeria, with corruption, and without corruption. And I can authoritatively tell you, from experience, that things are not well here. We are the ones to make things well, not "God". We are the ones to do the work by using our talents, knowledge, hardwork, sans corruption. "We are the ones we are waiting for." -Barack Obama. And we are here.

Stop waiting. And start doing, yes, with whatever you have. Focus on yourself. Become a better you. Be more competent, less corrupt. Think creatively, innovatively. Change certain things in your life. Be more financially prudent, less wasteful. Begin to lay the foundation for your family generational wealth. You do not know how? Go and learn. Let the heaven rest. "God" is not deaf.

This is a parable: If you claim that you have access to plenty water, why is that unwanted fire still burning under your rooftop? You keep bragging about your unlimited access to, not just water, but the cleanest, yet, the fire is still burning.

Your water is better than his, cleaner than his, you keep saying. Yet, the fire under your rooftop is still burning. Is it not the smoke from it, the smoke of discomfort, of disappointment, of dejection wafting up to the sky for all to see?

Look very well. His water that you called dirty has quenched his unwanted fire. It is no longer burning. He is at peace with himself because he has peace under his rooftop.

Bros, who cares about your water that you called the cleanest when it could not quench the unwanted fire under your own rooftop?

Ideals are good. But practicality is what always matters. And the usefulness of water, whether clean or dirty, in this case, should be the effectiveness of it in quenching unwanted fire, either under one's rooftop, or the rooftops of friends and family. "God" is indeed not deaf.

Every human has innate strengths, raw talents. But it has to be developed either through proper upbringing or self-development. But some people have been classically conditioned to think that they cannot do what they have the potential to do. Ultimately, they've learned how to be helpless. "Learned Helplessness"

What Is Learned Helplessness? "Learned helplessness occurs when an animal is repeatedly subjected to an aversive stimulus that it cannot escape. Eventually, the animal will stop trying to avoid the stimulus and behave as if it is utterly helpless to change the situation. Even when opportunities to escape are presented, this learned helplessness will prevent any action. While the concept is strongly tied to animal psychology and behavior, it can also apply to many situations involving human beings. When people feel that they have no control over their situation, they may also begin to behave in a helpless manner.
This inaction can lead people to overlook opportunities for relief or change." **By Kendra Cherry.**

"Only God knows" is a statement of ignorance. It is the same thing as saying, "I don't know". And, there is nothing wrong with not knowing as long as it becomes a catalyst for learning.
"Oluwa a ko wa mo se" "God will teach us how to do it." This statement is untrue. It is those who do not know how, or do not want, to learn that continue to use it as extension of "only God knows."

Those who know how to learn, and want to learn, will continuously use their innate intelligence to acquire pertinent knowledge, either by critical thinking/reasoning, research, or simply listening to the people that already know.

If your culture or religion has taught you how to be helpless, it is time to break free of that "learned helplessness" and replace it with "can do" attitude.

When someone walks in the center of "God's" will, his/her steps will be ordered. How do we know "God's " will? We have so many custodians of "God's" will. But we can use reverse reasoning to arrive at what many may regard as true.

If it is true that if someone walks in the center of "God's" will, his/
steps will be ordered, then it will also be true that someone with
ordered steps is walking in the center of "God's" will. By seeing
his/her ordered life, and not one in disarray, we will know that
someone is walking in the center of "God's" will. Not so? I always
maintain that fruits are the best indicator of what type
a tree is.

Then, wanting an ordered life is not something to pray for. It
ought to be a desire, backed up by striving to do the right things
the right way, if not in all things, in most things, if not all the time,
most of the time.

 It is everyone that will carry his/her own cross. And, a sick man
that keeps taking fake drugs may never get well." God" is not deaf.

Look at Nigeria. We can indeed tell a tree by the fruits it bears.

CHAPTER 2

WHAT IS A MYSTIC?

In the first chapter, I called myself a mystic. I know a lot of people may not know what a mystic is. First of all, let me define what mysticism is. Mysticism is the belief in the possibility of attaining direct communion with Ultimate Reality or knowledge of spiritual truths as by meditation.

However, for me, this is no longer a belief. It is now an experience. I sparingly use beliefs these days.

A mystic is one who professes to undergo profound spiritual experiences.

I began to tag myself as a mystic when a silent voice surfaced in my mental realm and began to teach and guide me. It was the voice that introduced me to the idea of verification, even before I studied the scientific method.

What is a Modern Mystic?

A modern mystic is a mystic who applies the scientific method to his or her spiritual experiences and thereby produces useful practical knowledge that has applicability in concrete reality. A modern mystic, by extension, is also a pragmatic mystic.

This is why I always insist that I must prove, verify all things. It is also the reason why I declared that "ideals are good but practicality is what always matters."

In relating to me, forget what you have read in books about mysticism. I have forgotten all I read about it. I only use what I have experienced, the part that is practical, the part that has added value, spice to my life.

The Pragmatic Mystic

It is very clear to me that I have a system that works, relatively, for me. I do not covet other people's system. And neither do I import that of others. Think of me as being spiritually independent and interdependent.

After my inculcated belief system collapsed, I began to painstakingly rebuild another one. I relied heavily on experiences, observations, reasoning, and verifications. Of course I had help. There is that silent voice in the abyss of my thoughts that always teaches, thrills, taunts.

Yes, sometimes it taught. Sometimes it thrilled. And sometimes it taunted. But it ultimately guided me away from my corrupt ways by steering me towards striving to do the right things the right way, in most things, and if not at all times, most of the time.

Is this inspiration, revelation, divination? It does not matter your choice of word. One thing that is certain is: It is spiritual guidance.

Yes, you can call it whatever you want. It does not matter to me. After all, a rose called by any name will still smell the same way. It is still teaching, thrilling, and taunting when the need calls for it.

Why do you think I continue to live, love and laugh? I am not hurting. And I am not hating. I am healed. And I continue to enjoy the simple pleasures of life. Ko ju be na lo fa. It is not more than that.

The following is a poem I wrote describing this voice in my abyss of thought.

Union.
It comes. It helps.
Does it plan to stay?

If it stays,
that will be good.
If it leaves,
it will be missed.
It spreads love.
It tells the truth.
It is fair, and
it makes me laugh.
It thrills, it teaches.
Sometimes it taunts.
It makes friend with Time.
It milks Time
for all Time's worth.
It always speaks
with a silent voice.
A silent voice
only I can hear.
Sometimes it is not working,
It takes a break, then,
a pen feels like a shovel,
a blank paper looks like an
unploughed piece of land.
The well of thoughts
runs dry. And I wait,

and wonder and ponder.
Then it comes.

I had a dream in 1979, 38 years ago. And I still remember it vividly as if it was yesterday. It is one of those dreams that stay fresh in your mind, that one is unable to forget.

In that dream, I was supposed to go and speak to my father. But I must go through two men who were manning the gate to his house. On getting to his house, the two men manning the gate were busy arguing passionately and were unaware that I was around. I slipped pass them, went into my father's room, spoke to him and he spoke to me.

The next morning, my grandfather woke me up from my dream around 6:00am for the mandatory morning prayers. I had gone to Sagamu Ogun State, Nigeria to spend my two weeks annual leave from Nigerian
Airways where I was working at the time. I woke up quite alright but I did not get up. I simply told my grandfather that I was not a Christian anymore. The old man could not believe his ears. So he repeated himself and I repeated myself.

Then what I said dawned on him. He simply said, "May God forgive you." And I simply said, "amen."

I did not understand this dream and my subsequent action until 1996, 19 years ago, while I was in deep meditation. The dream came back to my mind. It was vivid. And the silent voice in my abyss of thought explained that the two men I saw standing guard at the gate of my father represented Christianity and Islam, my father represented "God" and my speaking directly with my father represented my eventual evolution as a mystic. 'God' is not deaf.

Few years ago, I think it was 2015 if I am not mistaken, someone said, "I have wanted to ask Mr Fayemi this. Why does he always describe himself as a 'mystic'? From all appearance his aphorisms are more sage, wise, than mystical. Just wondering. Or the mystical side is shielded from us - the uninitiated!".

And I responded:

"I describe myself as a mystic, modern mystic to be precise (I use the scientific method), and not the type you read in books, but a mystic nonetheless, because the source of my writings is a silent voice in my abyss of thoughts.

I call It "Something that Speaks but is not Seen" A mystic, it has been said, is fundamentally a philosopher". I don't have any religion. However, I have evolved into a mystic. And a mystic is fundamentally a philosopher. I do not really attach a label to myself. I simply live, love, unfold, evolve. And when the bell tolls, as it eventually must, I would love to have become the best that I could have become. Hence I must continually strive for change, for growth.

This is also what someone said to me: you are really a great pragmatic philosopher of our time. I want you to step down on religious issues. Though you are entitled to your opinion. It is a free world. Good day"

And this is my response to him: "What you just said is akin to telling Toyota to step down the production and marketing of Lexus because you prefer BMW. Think about it. We lost our foundation when we began to import other people's foundational thoughts in the guise of beliefs."

CHAPTER 3

HOW AND WHEN I EVOLVED INTO A MYSTIC

In December of 1993, I realized that I was on life's dead end. I knew that I had to change my illegal lifestyle, my illegal way of making money. But I did not change fast enough. The consequences of not changing fast enough became my era of trial and tribulation, which is a subject of another book.

During this era of trial and tribulation, which spanned about eleven years, I began to change my ways. I vowed not to ever take part in any illegal activity. I began to retrain myself and invested my time in personal development. This was between 1994 and 1996.

In 1996, my brother, Niyi, sent me two books. One of the books was "The Prince" by Niccolo Machiavelli. The second one was "The Art of Dreaming" by Carlos Castaneda. In the book, "Art of Dreaming", I read that someone could set up his own dream.

Really?

That night, before I slept off, I decided to set up my own dream. I wished to dream about my children. And I truly dreamed about one of my children, Shola.

In the dream, I saw Shola sitting on a fence. She was undecided whether to be on this side of the fence or the other side. Her teeth were very dirty. She appeared unkept. Then I woke up from the dream. Okay. So it is indeed possible for someone to set up his own dream.

When I woke up the next morning, I called Shola's grandmother to find out how my daughter was doing.

"Hi ma", I said.

"Koolie, am glad that you called. The Department of Child Welfare is looking for Traci. They are trying to take her children away from her because, they said, she was not taking good care of the children."

Wow.

My dream was very close to reality.

The next morning I went to the Christian chaplain at the chapel near me. A "chaplain is a minister, such as a priest, pastor, rabbi, imam or lay representative of a religious tradition, attached to a secular institution such as a hospital, prison, military unit, school, police department, university, or private chapel." Wikipedia.

I explained my experience to the chaplain, who incidentally happened to have a master's degree in psychology. He told me that the book I read was fiction. Okay. But how fictitious could it be if I could do as it said and it worked?

When he realised I was not going to take no for an answer, he said he could bring me a book that would teach me how my dream would not come true again.

This man was not getting it. Here I was, trying to learn more about my experience and this man was saying something else.

Finally, he told me he would bring a book on Christian meditation for me. And that was the first time I heard anything about meditation.

The first book the chaplain brought, "The Other Side of Silence: Meditation for the Twenty-First Century by Morton T. Kelsey", taught me how to meditate. However, it tried to guide me to focus my mind on stories from the bible. My mind, feeling like it was being programmed, rebelled.

I went back to the chaplain and he brought another book for me: "The Experience of Insight" by Joseph Goldstein. I found this book insightful and liberating. It taught me two types of meditation: choice-less awareness and directed awareness.

In choice-less awareness, one simply sit in meditation, concentrating on one's breathing, and let whatever comes to come. But in directed awareness, one focuses on something in particular, like a vexing problem that needs to be solved, a concept in need of a deeper understanding etc.

Within one week of learning meditation, my inner life came alive. I began to see images in my meditation. And my intuition accelerated.

Sometimes after, I was in meditation and I saw a clock. The long hand of the clock ran and stopped at twelve and the short hand ran and stopped at three. Intuition said it was 3:00pm. Then I saw two police officers taking this African American guy that I usually play chess with, away in handcuffs.

I came out of meditation. The time was around 11am. I went looking for the roommate of the guy I just saw being led away in handcuffs. He was from Granada. And to him, my name was Africa. I told him what I just saw in my meditation. We then went our separate ways.

Unknown to Granada and me, his African American roommate had a problem with some guys out of New York and they decided to beat him up. Once he became aware of this, he quietly made a call to the police officers and requested to be taken into protective custody for his safety. It was exactly 3:00pm when he was led away, in handcuffs, to protective custody.

At another time, I lied down on my bed and covered myself from head to toe with a bed-sheet. I got into meditation and shortly after, a guy named Alvin came in. He was cooking for the two of us and I knew he came to pick up my bowl. Before he spoke, I told him to pick my bowl on top of my locker. He did, and he left. Soon after I finished my meditation and uncovered myself. That was when the new experience dawned on me: how did I know it was Alvin that came in when my eyes were closed and I had a bed-sheet covering me from head to toe?

Hmmmmmm

However, sometimes, instead of seeing images in my meditation, a complete sentence would come out of my silent mind. Some of these sentences are: "Half book of half-truths." "Ideals are good but practicality is what always matter." "Go through the same channel" etc.
I have since made "ideals are good but practicality is what always matter" my personal motto.

During another meditation session, a profound, liberating sense of freedom from within erupted from the depth of my being. This feeling is akin to the feeling one feels after a rope tying one down is let loose. Joyously, I began to say to myself, "I am free! I am free!"

Wow.

Dark Nights of the Soul.

In the same 1996, I went through my dark nights of the soul, my "coldest winter ever."

For about a week, I could not sleep well. I was very miserable. Depression took the thrill, the joy, the sweet out of my life.

Things that I had done in the past, some that I could not consciously remember, came to my mind. The consequences of those things I have done also came to my mind.

They joined together like siamese twin. Amazing.
It was like watching a movie to see its climax. I obtain my knowledge that "I always reap what I sow" from this inner experience.

That was when it downed on me that I was the one, through my thinking, my actions, my relationship with others, that manufactured my negative consequences.

Upon that realisation, like a fog, misery lifted, leaving in its wake my customary inner joy and peace. That was when I vowed to always strive to do the right things, the right way, at all times, in all things.

Now, because misery has fled from me, I am constantly bubbling, even with less money, even in PHCN-imposed darkness. Can't you feel me ni?

CHAPTER 4

WHAT IS GOD?

Is there something called "God"? Can a two-way communication take place between humans and God? Does "Something that Speaks But is Not Seen" reside in the human minds? Can one know his/her purpose in life? Is it possible to harness dreams to a point that they become fertile source of creativity?

I have explored all these and much more with meditation. I have moved beyond beliefs into the realm of knowing. The concept of "God" can be explored within modern context, without importation of ideology, without tall tales of antiquity, with the aim of fostering creativity.

I may like or not like what others say "God" is. But I cannot dispute what they say. I do not have enough experiential knowledge to do that. As for me. God is unknowable. The answer I got to the question, "What is God?", from my probing in meditation was, "God is unknowable. But some of his? Its? manifestations that may be unknown at some point in time can be made known by those that are spiritually/mentally awakened." From that point onward, I stopped confusing "the man pointing to the moon for the moon.". I simply listen, in silence, to "Something that Speaks But is not seen", a silent voice in my abyss of thoughts. A voice that thrills, taunts, teaches. I subject all thoughts from this source to the verification process while not ignoring a caveat that came from the same source that, "Ideals are good but practicality is what always matters."

I embarked on an "inward journey" in 1996. I wanted to know "What is God", among other things. The journey is still ongoing. And, the answer I got to the question, in 1997, was "God is unknowable. But some of his manifestations can be made known by the mentally or spiritually awakened ones." This is the totality of my knowledge about what "God" is.

I do not argue the existence or non-existence of "God". I leave that for the "experts", which majority of Nigerians are, anyway. My focus is on actions/inactions and corresponding verifiable results. I am not moved by mere claims. I have to see the manifestation of the Real Thing in the quality of life people are living.

As a pragmatic mystic, I only focus on the practicality of the idea. I neither gain nor lose by arguing for or against "God" concepts. What is it that I can do or gain by shouting on top of my lungs that

"God" exist! You must believe as I believe!" "God" is not Deaf!"? The people that did so, or continue to do so, did it, are doing it to dominate, to colonize. What is my own whether you believe in one "God" or many "Gods" or not? What competitive advantage do I gain apart from the domination and colonization that I already mentioned? And I am neither into domination nor colonization.

My motivation is fueled by the desire to ignite my compatriots' critical, creative, and innovative thinking ability so that we can unshackle our archaic, colonized minds.

I wish we can be humble enough to know that we do not truly know what or who "God" is. Simply repeating what we have read, or what some other people told us about "God" is not true knowledge. And until we admit that, we all will be wallowing in our mental arrogance of thinking we know what we truly do not know.

How come there is an inverse correlation between our people's knowledge of "God" and production/progress if they truly know what and who their "God" is? Those who know better do better.

Once the humility to admit triumph over the arrogance, the tyranny of certainty, we will all realize, like I did as a mystic, that what we are actually wrestling with are ideas about "God". Ideas that may be true or false. Ideas that may be good or bad. Ideas that may have the seed of mediocrity in them or that may have potential for excellence.

And, like St. Augustine said, "Faith is to believe what you do not see; the reward of this faith is to see what you believe.'

Majority of Nigerians lay claim to one faith or the other. But, have the majority of us not been praying ceaselessly in the last two years for the betterment of this country? Can anyone produce the proof of what has truly improved since then?

It is not that we are not praying enough. It is because majority of us are not doing the right things, the right way, in all things, and at all times. Clarity seems to be a scarce commodity in this part of the world. Prejudice and partiality reign supreme.

A lot of people know what/who "God" is, with certainty. I do not. I approach the concept of God with ignorance, with curiosity, with open mind. They approach it with beliefs they have elevated to the level of knowledge. And, consequently, suffer from tyranny of certainty. I am a knower who rely heavily on reasoning, logic and verification. They are believers who rely on faith. I produce my own ideology. I do not import what I can produce. After all, a mystic is fundamentally a philosopher. They import their own, setting the foundation for ceaseless imports.

We are different by light years! My system accommodates all others because "in my father's house, there are many mansions there." Theirs does not. They insist that their way is the only way. Who is arrogant and who is not? Who is amenable to change and who is not?

The more I try to explain myself to some people, to make them realize I may be different from them, the more they are resisting to understand me because I do not fit into their belief system, which, unfortunately, has become their prejudice. Clarity, thus, continues to elude them. And some people still wonder why bad things happen to "good" people?

Prejudice!

Prejudice, the act of prejudging people is bad. Be aware. Desist. And, get a cure by cultivating a beginner's mind. What is labelled "beginner's mind" here has since evolved into "learning mode". A "beginner's mind" "refers to having an attitude of openness, eagerness, and lack of preconceptions when studying a subject, even when studying at an advanced level, just as a beginner in that subject would."

In addition, instead of prejudice, a lot of people need to develop empathic listening skills. "Empathic listening (also called active listening or reflective listening) is a way of listening and responding to another person that improves mutual understanding and trust."

Anyone that wants to gain clarity must begin by striving to do the right things the right way. No effective decision can be made without clarity. And, decisions made without clarity always lead to frustration, dejection and unfulfillment.

Mahalia Jackson, an American gospel singer, wrote the following. And I passionately agree with her. "We must demonstrate what we know about God in the way we think, talk, walk, and live. God is peace. God is strength. God is mercy. God is forgiving. God is all knowing, all powerful, abundant, radiant life. God is Love. To know God is to be like Him. All else is a figment of your imagination."

The earth has numerous valuable minerals buried within its core. This is a fact. Nigeria has crude oil buried within her belly. That's why our chief dollars earner is the export of crude oil. This is a fact. So, if anyone claims that the land in his backyard is full of gold, the abundant gold he possesses will naturally suffice to validate his claim. Not so?

So, as a pragmatic mystic, if anyone claims to me that he or she has the knowledge of "God", he or she must be brimming with a manifestation of "God". Whatever he/she says "God" is must exude, not merely from his/her mouth, but from his/her character, in his/her life in abundant supply. This, folks, is also a fact.

To claim the knowledge of "God", with nothing to show, is downright delusional. "Blessed are the pure in heart, for they shall see God." Is your heart pure?

"God" is not inside a book. But stories about "God" are. We can tell a tree by the fruits it bears. "God is not deaf".

In the Nigerian context, whether you see the cup as half empty or half full, the truth is majority of us have half cup of "water" to drink. How you see it may not quench your thirst. However, being contented with drinking half cup of "water" may suffice. And I stand to be counted with those that are contented with drinking half cup of "water".

Albert Einstein was right when he said, "The world we have created is a product of our thinking. It cannot be changed without changing our thinking." It is axiomatic that the Nigeria we have created is a product of our thinking, actions and inactions. And it cannot be changed without changing our thinking and actions. "God" will come and change it? Wake up and smell the coffee. That idea about "God" is for the mentally, psychologically and spiritually undeveloped people.

It may have been our parents' fault for giving us ineffective leadership and beliefs, but it is now our fault, for hanging on to what is clearly not working, for not changing.

We have descended to the depth where lies are more comforting than truths. We need to soar to the height where truths are more comforting than lies. How do we know the truths? They work......even if not on the short run......on the long run. "Faith is to believe what you do not see; the reward of this faith is to see what you believe:- St. Augustine. Is our faith manifesting in our lives? Or is it just lifeless ideas to be debated with people of other faith, or nonbelievers?

We all know that there is relative order in the universe. Let us assume that this order is a manifestation of "God". So, anyone who claims to have knowledge of God, or has a relationship with" Him", must naturally have order in his or her life. Order, which is now the fruit, is how we can tell the tree, which is the knowledge of "God", or a relationship with "Him".

And for me, once anyone has the fruit, whether he/she believes in" God" or not, I automatically know that he/she has done the right things the right way. Or else the fruit won't be his/hers.

Ordered thinking is a prerequisite for ordered life. Dwelling on mere tree when one already has the favorable and desirable fruit is unprogressive.

The first step towards creating order is self-discipline, self-control, self-denial, coupled with "let your yes be yes, and let your no be no." When we have disciplined ourselves up to the point where "doing the right things the right way" becomes second nature, creating order, even in the midst of chaos, in our lives becomes inevitable.

Order, whether created and sustained with peace, love and justice, or created and sustained with almighty power, is still order. But I personally prefer the one created and sustained with peace, love, and justice.

Nigeria is a very peculiar country. All sort of fraudsters use the name of "God", mostly in vain, in contravention of one of the 10 Commandments.

Alarm in my head goes off when people use the name of "God" where it is not necessary. I become more cautious. For example: If I ask a mechanic if he knows what is wrong with my car and he says, Olorun a ko wa mo se, ("God" will teach us how to do it) I know I am in for a ride of trial and error.

Attaching the name of "God" to incompetence does not produce competence. Attaching the name of "God" to corrupt proceeds is a crude attempt to show authentic blessing.

Focused studies, coupled with disciplined practice, is what brings competence to life.

Doing the right things the right way is the only path to righteousness, uprightness, not the unscrupulous attachment of "God's" name to irrelevance. Be warned.

The clearest sign to know who has "God" in his/her life is the manifestation of the "fruits of the spirit" in that person's life. And the clearest sign that one is seeking "God" is a lifestyle that reeks of uprightness, a lifestyle that is infused with diligence. It was true that one can tell a tree by the fruits it bears. It is still true now. And, it was true that the manifestation of love is the presence of "God". It is still true now. A lifestyle of corruption, of hating on others, is not compatible with "God".

I constructively criticize religion, not antagonize it. All religions are supposedly rooted in righteousness. And as a mystic, I must embrace righteousness, and abstain from all form of evil. If you see my constructive criticism as negative, check yourself, constructively. You may be a negative person cloaking yourself as a religious person. Or.....you may either be sincerely wrong, or zealously misguided.

The proliferation of "adulterated doctrines" in our midst is a manifestation of corruption. Corruption and uprightness are Not compatible. If you like, pray ceaselessly and fast two hundred days. At least the rest of us will have enough to eat by your abstinence.

I am for the type of religion that fused rights and obligations together. As a pragmatic mystic, it is pleasant to my soul. It is the delusional type that proclaims rights but disdains obligations that I find odious. How can you come to me, bragging about your "God's" promises to you when you are clearly failing in upholding" His" commandments?

Religious beliefs, without uprightness is like a car without engine. It will take you nowhere but keep you in one spot. Or why do you think the majority here fail to live satisfying lives? That nagging, persistent feeling of inadequacy is a clear sign of spiritual malnourishment.

Change your ways.

Spiritual growth requires that we go beyond books, beyond the known, into the realm of unknown, if we desire to push the frontier of civilization towards growth, towards enduring happiness and lasting success. If we do otherwise, we will stagnate.

In December of 2016, I asked the following question: Does "God" really care who suffers and who doesn't? I could not answer this question at that time. But I think I can answer that question now: It is not for "God" to care who suffers and who does not. It is for the individual to use his/her dominion over most things to make sure he or she does not suffer, by doing the right things the right way.

Many years ago, a man told me that to get anything, all we had to do was claim it by faith and that thing would be ours. Just like that? I of course disagreed with him. He scoffed at my formula of doing the right things the right way to get what we wanted. As at today, the man still lives in penury, still claiming by faith, and still waiting on the good lord to do wonders in his life. "Oluwa a se iyanu" Caveat: claiming anything by faith, without doing the required work, is surely an exercise in futility. Faith without work was dead in antiquity. Faith without work is dead now. "God" is not deaf.

Okey Ndibe wrote: "Has it ever been heard or seen that God built roads, swept streets....dug boreholes, investigated corruption, chased down murderers? Now, if God has not done these things for any people, why do Nigerians disturb the serenity of heaven with petitions for divine intervention in matter that they, and they alone, ought to handle?" God is not deaf.

Quite a lot of people have said, are saying, "God" works in mysterious ways." Yes, that may be technically true. But we have to work, diligently, ceaselessly, to unravel that mystery. If we do not, and we have not, we will continue to live in ignorance, in perpetual backwardness.

The definition of mystery is "something that is difficult or impossible to understand." And, the definition of ignorance is "lack of knowledge or information." Spot the difference? Is mystery not synonymous with ignorance? Is unraveling mystery not the fulcrum on which modern knowledge turns?

In 2014, someone said to me: "the magnitude of God is given in our despair. The uneducated and the downtrodden are his favourite."

Really? This was amazing. Wasn't it? So I said: to him, "So how did the downtrodden, the uneducated, those despairing, become God's favorite when they are lacking in basic necessities, wallowing in abject poverty while their corrupt, inept leaders wine and dine and ride in jets?"

He responded: "Ever read the bible? Difficulties have a way of making us look to God and seek his face....not Facebook theology".

This was getting real interesting, I thought.

Then I countered: "Ever heard of slavery and colonization and PHCN-induced darkness with heat and mosquitoes? You still need more difficulties? Be for real. I am getting to understand why the black race is very much behind."

Beliefs and life experience ought to match. If they do not, then we may be lying to ourselves

Your believing, or non-believing, in "God" has no relevance to me. It does not produce any verifiable competitive advantage. However, your 'doing the right things, the right way, in all things, and at all times", regardless of your believing or non-believing in" God", that is what is sacrosanct to me.

The "fruits" are still the best way for me to tell whether the "tree" is fertile or barren. "God" is not deaf.

Some people have said that "the voice of the people is the voice of "God." Some have said that "one with God is a majority." Can these two sentences, if they are true, coexist together? How relevant is any of them to our present predicament in Nigeria? Is it the majority's thoughts/actions/inactions subjecting us to our present privations? Or is it the thoughts/actions/inactions of the minority responsible?

And, since" God" is not deaf, why is it that the prayer of the majority is largely not answered? Please use critical thinking and not prejudice to sincerely answer these questions for yourself. The answers to these questions is the subject of another book coming out soon.

What is critical thinking? Critical thinking is "the objective analysis and evaluation of an issue in order to form a judgement". -www.coursehero.com
And, "skills that we need in order to be able to think critically are

varied and include observation, analysis, interpretation, reflection, evaluation, inference, explanation, problem solving, and decision making."-www.skillsyouneed.com

In my opinion, Mother Teresa manifested "God's" love. She was a success in my book, a huge success. Yet, she was not reported to be a rich woman. She neither owned fleet of cars, nor did she operate her own private plane. But because she loved what she did, she did it passionately, effectively, religiously.

Who is Mother Teresa? "Mother Teresa MC, known in the Catholic Church as Saint Teresa of Calcutta[6] (born Anjezë Gonxhe

Bojaxhiu Albanian: [a'?? z?'g? nd?? b? ja'd?iu]; 26 August 1910 – 5 September 1997), was an Albanian-Indian Roman Catholic nun and missionary.She was born in Skopje (now capital of the Republic of Macedonia), then part of the Kosovo Vilayet in the Ottoman Empire. After having lived in Macedonia for eighteen years, she moved to Ireland and then to India, where she lived for most of her life.

In 1950, Teresa founded the Missionaries of Charity, a Roman Catholic religious congregation, which in 2012 consisted of over 4,500 sisters and was active in 133 countries. They run homes for people dying of HIV/AIDS, leprosy and tuberculosis; soup kitchens; dispensaries and mobile clinics; children's and family counselling programmes; orphanages; and schools. Members must adhere to the vows of chastity, poverty, and obedience, as well as a fourth vow, to give "wholehearted free service to the poorest of the poor.

Teresa was the recipient of numerous honours, including the 1962 Ramon Magsaysay Peace Prize and 1979 Nobel Peace Prize. She was canonised(recognised by the church as a saint) on 4 September 2016, and the anniversary of her death, 5 September, was made her feast day.

A controversial figure both during her life and after her death, Teresa was widely admired by many for her charitable works. She was both praised and criticised for her views against abortion. She was criticised for the poor conditions in the houses for the dying she ran. Her authorised biography was written by Indian civil servant Navin Chawla and published in 1992, and there are other books and films about her." From Wikipedia

CHAPTER 5

CONVERSATION WITH "GOD"

God": "Even though you were raised as a Christian, you are very ignorant of the other world's religions. Go back and study all those religions. Aro meta ki nda obe nu. At least study the three major ones in your country."

Me: "The three major ones? But I know of only Christianity and Islam."

God: Chuckling, "Don't you know Ifa is a part of the traditional African religion?"

Me: "Of course I do not know."

God: "Ifa is the oracular deity in the original Yoruba religion. And your lineage used to be Ifa priests but abandoned it for Christianity"

Me: "But why study all religions when I am not even religious?"

God: "You have to learn what is known already. Then come back later to learn what is unknown."

Hmmmmmm.

I found out that the world has over 4000 religions!

So, I studied all the World's major religions, about ten in number, but refused to study the Ifa religion. Who wanted to go back to archaic religion? Not me.

Growing up, I had been inculcated with the belief that those practicing the traditional African religions were idol worshipers, that they worship Satan. The more I thought about this childhood conditioning, the more my resolution not to study the Ifa religion.

Then depression descended. Clinical depression, not mere sadness and sorrow. Life lost its pleasant allurement.

Naturally, I sought the psychologist's assistance. This was in Allenwood, Pennsylvania, United State

After several hours of counselling, the American psychologist, who was white and a Christian, advised me to honour the unseen voice's instruction. He gave me a clean bill of psychological health by saying there was nothing wrong with me apart from cognitive dissonance. He said my Subjective Reality ought to be in Alignment with my Objective Reality.

Okay. So I studied the Ifa religion. And I found it not to be compatible with my evolved mind.

Thereafter, like a fog, the depression lifted, leaving inner peace and inner joy in its place.

But......

I learned two vital concepts from my study of Ifa:

The first one is, eni ti o ba se otito ju ni Ifa ma ngbe. Ifa favours the most honest.

The second one is that the Ifa priest, as a prerequisite to making any sacrifice, must offer a sacrifice to Esu. This stems from the belief that Olodumare (God) has empowered Esu to cause disturbance anywhere good things are being done. So, to prevent

Esu from coming to disturb his good sacrifice, the priest "give
unto Ceaser what is Ceaser's".

Of course this sounds logical to me as a concept, even if not as a
practice. And I have since incorporated that concept into
my thinking and implanted it into my behavior.

I have since "sacrificed" all the thinking and behavior that
prevented the doing the right things the right way, if not in all
things, in most things, if not at all times, most of the time.
This, to me, is true salvation.

Conversation with "God"
Year 2000

"God": "Stop praying."

Me: "Sop praying? You must not be "God" Everyone that believes
in "God" prays."

So I kept on praying ceaselessly.

A year passed.

"God": "Your prayers are not being answered."

That was true. None of my prayer in the preceding year was
answered.

Hmmmm.

"God": "You are reaping what you sowed. No amount of prayer
can change that."

"God": "While you are here, I will teach you how to live a lifestyle, one contrary to the one that brought you here, a lifestyle of striving to do the right things the right way, in all things, and at all times."

I wrestled with this for a while. I got angry. I even cursed "God" out. I told "Him" to take "His" miserable life back, that I did not want it again.

I was depressed for a period of time. Not ordinary sorrow, but the type that required taking antidepressants for.
Then the lessons of life began by the silent voice in my abyss of thoughts. And the depression lifted, the enjoyment of simple pleasures of life that I had taken for granted resumed. I went on to master "ordinary humans emotions" and the thinking that produces them. That was how I acquired my emotional equilibrium. Peace came first, followed by contentment. My heart then became a fertile ground for love to bloom. You can now dance "Shoki" inside my belly, frolicking in the juice of my joy. That was seventeen years ago. That was how, and when I stopped praying. That was when disappointment, frustration sadness/sorrow fled. That was when I truly began to live, love and laugh.

Look at me now. Look at me again. Don't you see how my "outrageous misfortune" became "God's" blessing in disguise?

Conversation with "God".
Year 2000.

"God": You are afraid to live in Nigeria because you do not want to suffer."

Me: "Yes. After all these years in the US, I cannot cope with that suffering and smiling of no light, no water, no good roads etc."

"God": "With your vow that you will no longer get involved in corrupt practices, I can guarantee you that you will not suffer in Nigeria.. That is where your purpose in life is. That is where you will live a life that has meaning."

I am writing this book in 2017. My pact with "God" in 2000 is still going strong. The sun does not "smite me during the day, nor the moon by night." Ideals are good. But practicality is what always matter. And obligations and entitlement are irrevocably linked.

Conversation with "God."
2016

"God": "All of you in Nigeria are victims of circumstances."

Me: "What do you mean?"

"God:" "You are all victims of corruption, both predators and preys."

Me: "So, none of us is to be blamed for corruption then?"

"God": "None. But you all cannot have a vibrant country with corruption."

Me: "I do not understand. None of us is to be blamed for corruption. Yet we cannot "get there from here"?

"God": Yes. To "get there from here, the 3R must be embedded in your culture."

Me: "What is the 3R?"

"God":   "Remorsefulness.   Repentance.   Restitution."

"God": Tell all Nigerians, both the predators and the preys, that they must change their ways if they want to enjoy the fruits of their labours.

"God": "Remind them that the prayer of those who do not follow the law is an abomination in the eyes of "God".

I have always maintained that prayer is an exercise in futility if not coupled with "doing the right things the right way, in all things, and at all times."

So, to those who think I am wrong, that they can achieve what their hands do not work for, by simply enlisting the power of prayer, how did we arrive at this junction where the Naira is at its weakest and the prices of essential commodities have since doubled, in spite of our collective prayer?

How? How? How?

Prayer is not the solution to our national ailments. Neither is fasting. Forget tithes paying too. There is nothing holy in it. It is simply the payment one pays for importing the brand of thinking one cannot produce.

Having effective religious, political, traditional leaders who inspire, compel us to do the right things, the right way, in all things, and at all times is the solution. No one can plant corn and reap beans. No amount of praying and fasting can achieve that. "God" is not deaf.

A lot of religious folks need to get their acts together. If we say, let us do it, that we are the ones to do it. They will say, we cannot do anything without "God" and prayer. Then, when things don't get done, even with "God" and prayer, and we point out this obvious fact to them, they will come and say, let us leave "God" out of this. because "He" has given us the power to do it.

And, because of their ambivalence, born out of cognitive dissonance, whose grandparents are "classical conditioning" and "learned helplessness", most things do not get done. Most things do not work well. Yet, we continue to underachieve and overcelebrate. This is the true position of things now.

CHAPTER 6

WHAT IS FAITH?

aith is to believe what you do not see; the reward of this faith is to see what you believe.' St. Augustine.

Who is St. Augustine? According to Wikipedia, "Augustine of Hippo was an early Christian theologian and philosopher whose writings influenced the development of Western Christianity and Western philosophy. He was the bishop of Hippo Regius, located in Numidia."

I find his quote on faith very relevant to my experience. I have since discovered that a very thin line separates faith from delusion. Faith, of course, always works, always. But delusion never work, never.

A deluded person is always in a perpetual waiting mode for illusory promises. And I have seen people that have elevated delusion to the level of faith.

Faith is essentially to trust that something will happen and it does. Faith has truth as its foundation. Delusion is to trust that something will happen and it does not. It has lies as its foundation. There is a clear difference. The more one believes in something that is not true, the more stagnant one is going to become. It is as simple as ABC.

Defining of Delusion: Expecting, hoping,or praying for things that will never happen. Doing things the wrong way, yet expecting the right results is delusional. False beliefs that will never manifest in concrete reality is delusion. Unrealistic expectations are the children of delusion.

Delusion is dangerous. It impedes progress by directing efforts towards retrogressive projects. If you have been expending efforts, but without commensurate progress, take a test for detection of delusion.

Delusion can be mild or acute. I need to take a test for detection of delusion. Is mine mild or acute? I have been expending efforts for eight years, to bring about desirable change, but without commensurate progress. Is it not delusional to expect change from people that are unwilling or unable to change?

Faith without work is said to be dead. Prayer is an act of faith. It is not work. Beliefs are elements of faith. They are not work. Tithing, seeding, night vigils, pilgrimage to Mecca and Jerusalem etc are religious rituals. They are not work.

What, then, is this work that is so fundamental to making faith come alive? In modern language, it is the input-process-output model. This is the foundation of all things produced by humans. Those who have mastered, and continually implement the input-process-output model, succeed. Those who ignore it, fail.

What is input-process-output model?

Let's say you want to always have food in your house. Becoming a farmer will be one good option. Acquiring lands, farm helps, seedlings etc. are quintessential. They are your input. The actual cultivation of the land, weeding and watering, etc, these are your process.

Aha!

The harvest, the real reason behind your striving that is your output. Failing to go through the required necessary steps and praying ceaselessly is an exercise in futility. It is a clear sign of someone who does not love the truth.

And the reward for not loving the truth is: "And for this cause God shall send them strong delusion, that they should believe a lie: That they all might be damned who believed not the truth, but had pleasure in unrighteousness."

Ladies and gentlemen, stop your self-delusion. There is no substitute for doing the right things the right way. Stop chasing shadows. No one is known to ever catch one.

Creative, innovative thinking, meditation, researching, verification are some of the processes, the work required to bring good things to life!

Regardless of all our religious observance, If we do not have the love of truth, "God" will send us a strong dosage of delusion, and we will believe lies. Believing lies and acting on them waste time, efforts, with no favorable results.

In addition, because the mind does not have the capacity to know what is true or not, it is the responsibility of lovers of truth to test all things to ascertain their veracity before stamping anything as true.

There are three tests of truth.

One is the correspondence test. Let's say I received a bank alert for 100k yesterday. I did not know who sent it. And I did not tell anyone. And today, here you come, saying, did you get the alert for the 100k I sent you yesterday? That's an example of correspondence test. My experience corresponded with your utterance.

Another test of truth is coherence test. Let's say someone comes to you. And after bragging of how blessed he is, how his prayers are always being answered, how he even have 200k in his account right now, he begs you to give him transport money to go home.

Can you see that there is no coherence in his story. And consequently, the story, 9/10 cannot be true.

Ah!!!! As a pragmatic mystic, I love the pragmatic test of truth the most. Let's say I tell you that I can play piano. Won't it be easy for you to know that I can truly play piano if you simply give me the piano to play for you to see? I think it will be. Once you see me playing the piano, my claim that I can play piano has not only pass the pragmatic test, it has also pass the correspondence and coherence tests.

"Quench not the spirit, despise not prophecy. test all things....."
The truth always work. If most things are working well in our life, kudos to us. That is the clearest sign that we have mitigated delusion

The reason we put so much effort, so much commitment into any endeavour is to achieve desirable and favourable result, within reasonable time frame. If the effort, the commitment is coupled with the right and truthful knowledge, thinking/beliefs, it will yield the desired, favorable result. But if the effort, the commitment is coupled with half truths, lies, and delusions, the desired, favorable result will never come, leading to frustration, anger, and disappointment.

Get rid of delusion, and half-truths, outright lies will disappear, taking frustration, anger and disappointment with them.

CHAPTER 7

REFINED SPIRITUALITY

Spirituality simply means to go beyond the known, the seen, into the unknown, unseen. Vision is one of the derivatives of spirituality. And, it is common knowledge that vision and leadership are the two sides of the same coin. Therefore, because many of our so-called religious, political leaders constantly borrow their vision from foreign lands, we have effectively outsourced our leadership functions out to those foreign lands. These so-called leaders are mere followers, mere distributions of other people's visions. It is then no wonder that no meaningful and original mental production is going on here in our own clime. Those who import their "Gods" will also import their products.

Spirituality is the "inside-out" approach. You simply allow what is within you to unfold, without prejudice, with critical thinking, with constant verification. That, in my opinion, is the real "spiritual" growth. Is it not written that the kingdom of "God" is within you?

The core of any religion is spirituality. But most religionists are not into spirituality. Or to put it another way, spirituality, which is to transcend the physical, is not into them. Accurate vision is the clearest manifestation of true spirituality. Most religious houses have become the mansions of delusion, where strong delusion reigns as king. Is it not written that "God" "Himself" will send strong delusion to those who do not love the truth so that they can believe lies? How can anyone who does not prove, test, and verify all things claim to love the truth?

What a lot of people called interpretation is truly a distortion of the truth. True interpretation ought to match our shared reality. Accurate interpretation of reality brings contentment. Distortion of reality ultimately brings dissatisfaction. In the abundance of "water", some people are thirsty.

Largely, spiritual guidance is not inside books. It seeps directly into the human mind. And, it is not speaking in tongues. "Glossolalia or speaking in tongues, according to linguists, is the fluid vocalizing of speech-like syllables that lack any readily comprehended meaning, in some cases as part of religious practice in which it is believed to be a divine language unknown to the speaker." Those who know true spirituality, know this.

The clearest sign of true spirituality is accurately favorable and desirable vision, not the mindless repetition, like a parrot, of frozen truths that we currently have in front of us.

The truly guided, whether secular or spiritual, live an orderly life and not one in disarray. They live a contented life and not one of perpetual lacking, not one of unending dissatisfaction.

Repeating what happened over two thousand years ago, or merely repeating what has been written at any time is not what spirituality is about. Spiritual growth is quite different from religiosity. It is deeper, and it manifests in one's thinking and behavior. "Spiritual growth means advancing in all forms of conversation through deep understanding of knowledge which is devoid of delusion." You can call it mental or psychological growth. Different names, same manifestation. And spiritual growth is not about repeating ancient stories. It is about living a fulfilling life. it is about enjoying the "fruits of the spirit.". Mental/spiritual/psychological growth cannot be forced. It must naturally evolve. And without it, stagnation is natural.

Religious rituals, religious platitudes, do not produce the "fruits of the spirit". Upright living is still the most effective producer of verifiable "fruits". "The fruit of the Spirit is love, joy, peace, forbearance, kindness, goodness, faithfulness,"

It is possible to have a "tree" without "fruits". But it is not possible to have "fruits" without a "tree". So, shouldn't a prudent person use the "fruits" to identify a fertile "tree"? That is what I do. Show me the "fruits" and I will tell you how fertile the "tree" is. Remember a fruitless tree was cursed before. Right?

What some people tag "God's word" is what I tag "book talk".

Hear this:

Someone colonized us, gave us a book, and told us, "Here, this is what "God" says." And we believed it. And we programmed ourselves with what was written inside the book. That is neither spirituality nor thinking. That is, at best, called believing. When we get awakened and start thinking critically, we will actually know what spirituality is, what thinking is, and what programming is. And if lucky, we will know what spiritual guidance is. Religion and critical thinking are poles apart. And I guess most people go for the easier one.

But not me. I am awakened. I will go to the hospital when I am sick, not to the faith healers. And, as a responsible adult, I am the one to be blamed for all my wrongdoings, not "Satan". That is why I continually strive to do the right things the right way, in most things, most of the time, not alone, but with inner spiritual guidance, a silent voice in my abyss of thoughts, coupled with critical reasoning.

According to Shakespeare, a rose flower, called by any name, will still smell the same way. And "original", called by any name, will still produce the "fruits" of the "original". Think of Ragolis, Swan, Eva etc. They are all brand names selling water. However, water is water, whether in a cup, bowl, or bottle.

Let us open our hands, not our mouth, and look into our lives. Are we truly holding the "original"? Show me the "fruits of the spirit", the blessing by "God" of the works of your hands. In your life, show me love, joy, peace, gentleness, goodness, uprightness. Show me patience minus long-suffering, minus corruption. Show me, with your actions, the loving of your neighbors as yourself. And, if what you are holding is fake, and therefore nothing to write home about, then, it is time to unlearn, relearn, and start afresh.

That is a tough one, is it not?
In my own book, perpetual hopes cannot replace the actual blessings of holding the "original" in our hands. The lasting pleasant sweetness that comes from the "original" is a reward for possessing it. Who feels it knows it.

If you are a mere believer, or nonbeliever, please do not pass by and just keep going about your business without reading this page. It is definitely for you too even though some things are simply not for everybody.

And, if you are a knower, that is the more reason you can read on, if you will, and time permits. As a knower, you have the wherewithal to understand this page.

Anyone that claims Jesus Christ is God is not spiritually awakened. I repeat, anyone that claims that Jesus Christ is God is not spiritually awakened. Jesus himself said "Believest thou not that I am in the Father, and the Father in me? the words that I speak unto you I speak not of myself: but the Father that dwelleth in me, he doeth the works."

When one is spiritually awakened, he//she will know that there is a stage of spiritual growth that is called "union with God." During this stage of spiritual development, the Spirit of God dwells in the person that has gone through the discipline of becoming awakened and becoming enlightened. The spirit does not possess him/her. Instead, he/she possesses the spirit, and consequently lives uprightly, conscious of the presence of "God" in all utterances and deeds. He/she will effortlessly do the right things the right way, if not in all things, in most things, if not at all times, most of the time. Because he or she already knows that "God" is not deaf.

No matter how lofty a spiritual stage that is, it is wrong to confuse "the man pointing to the moon for the moon." Sitting a man on the throne of "God" is not spirituality. It is definitely not spiritual knowledge. It is religion, definitely religious doctrine.

As long as we are not well versed in the art of verification, delusion will always be our ally, and propagandists, demagogues, will always be our leaders, both politically and religiously. A demagogue is "a political leader who seeks support by appealing to popular desires and prejudices rather than by using rational argument."

It continues to baffle me when some people try to remove the intellect from spirituality. It is not supposed to be so. Yes, the intellect is inadequate to access spirituality, but it is required to understand it. Anyone trying to remove intelligence, the human faculty necessary for learning and understanding, and sometimes for dealing with new and trying situation, as we now have in Nigeria, is peddling delusion. And with delusion, the waiting period for manifestation is endless.

When we depart from our "own" where we could have evolved to be a leader, a producer, an exporter, and are are enmeshed in that of "others" where we will always be followers, consumers, importers, then we have effectively demonstrated that "a borrower will always be servant to the lender."

I assume that majority of Nigerians want the best in Life. We want good quality of life. And those of us that pray have been, and will earnestly be petitioning God to assist in this regard. But....God is not deaf.

The foundational thoughts/beliefs in the head of most people I know are fixed, not amenable to change, not to talk of creating new ones. We are stuck for now. And stagnation is the natural consequences.

But it does not have to be this way only if we can begin to think creatively, innovatively. It is erroneous to think that condition must be right to think right. Contrarily, it is the condition that is not right that motivates one to think about what to do to make things right. After all, necessity is said to be mother of invention. And adani loro, agbara lo fi ko ni. It is during adversity that certain strengths can be developed.

It may be delusional to make decisions without having corresponding power/resources to carry out the decisions. When our desires exceed our power/resources, our mind becomes susceptible to all sorts of negativity, delusion included. We leave ourselves open to manipulation by others offering perpetual promise of everlasting solution. Promises that are perpetual: just promises.

As an initial matter, we ought to shrink our desires to the limit of our power/resources. Then we try find creative ways to grow within the scope of our limitations. Simply put, we must cut coat according to your fabrics.

In spirituality the madman and the genius reside on the same island. However, there is a thin line separating the two. While a madman "seeing" motivates him to act, his actions lead to futility. The genius' "seeing" however motivates him to act in accordance with correct principles leading to the manifestation of the gifts of the spirituality. The scientific method can be used to guarantee that one doesn't cross that thin line into insanity(delusion). This is my experience. This is my type of spirituality

There is true spirituality which leads to enlightenment. An enlightened human knows right from wrong. Her/his actions are guided by conscience. He/she strives to continually treat others with a sense of fairness. And of course she/he abstains from all forms of evil. In addition, there is junk spirituality which stems from delusion. Anyone that practices junk spirituality, according to one of our books, " his/her toil will show no profit." In conclusion, we can "tell the tree by the fruits it bears".

Now, please analyse the following story and determine if it is junk or true spirituality. Judge if it is true guidance or the delusional one.

Sometimes in 2012, my phone rang early in the morning and I picked it up, even though I mostly do not pick up unknown number calls. It was from one of my cousins that I have not seen since 1977. The phone connection cut as soon as she identified herself and I called her back. She said she missed my dad, her uncle, and went to visit him. She said she had a spiritual message for me, that I should come over. But because I was not interested in her spiritual message, I said that I was not in Lagos. I told her to tell me her message on the phone. She said that I had a close friend, that I should not trust him, that if something is X, I should tell him it is Y. She said there was a family member on my mother side that was evil, that was out to revenge something done to her, that was now bent on taking revenge on me and my brother, that I should come for her to pray for me because she had the holy spirit in her. I told her that she was stupidly illogical, that by me telling my friend something was Y when it was X was in violation of my new policy of "let your yes be yes and your no be no", that by seeing any of my family as evil when there was no concrete proof, was to be malicious and evil myself. She splashed some more religious platitudes but I simply hung up the phone. Enough of wasting my valuable time in listening to complete nonsense and wasting my scare resources I used to call her back. In my opinion, I had labelled her behavior as exploitative, a clear manifestation of junk spirituality, unworthy for the truth seekers, and the preference of the delusional. My decision to be sincere and honest, not only to my friends, but also to all my associates, is irrevocable. I will rather label those who betray my trust as traitors than for them to label me as dishonest.

According to some people, erstwhile President Jonathan included, was quoted to have said that if not for the prayers of Nigerians, things could have been worse.

Hehehehehe.

What a clumsy statement coming from defective leadership and swallowed by even more defective followership. What a statement justifying mediocrity.. It is statement like this, believed by millions, that serves as an anchor weighing us down in the river of stagnation.

A symptom of defective leadership is when one gives value to valueless things, when one uses 20,000 Naira to purchase 17,000 Naira new notes in order to "spray" at parties.

Leadership and culture are the two sides to the same coin. Just as defective leadership will produce defective culture, defective culture will continually churn out defective leadership.

What we throw at life has a magical way of coming back to us. "God" is not deaf. One of the opportunity cost of our ceaseless, wasteful, religious/cultural celebrations is our deficient infrastructure! Believe it or not, it is up to you.

If it is true that majority of our so-called leaders are being led by others, then, is it not also true that we are practically followers of followers?

A quintessential of leadership is vision.

And, my knowledge tells me that first class vision comes directly into the human mind. But, the second, third class one can be found in books!

When we are ready to move away from cut and paste leaders, be it religious or cultural, by crafting our own ideology ourselves, by defining our own reality ourselves, then, we can truly begin our own journey towards independence, towards growth and progress.

Until then, we will continue to import, continue to over celebrate and underachieve. And our Naira will continue to weaken.

In the meantime, intelligent, serious-minded Nigerians need to put on their thinking cap. In the silence of their rooms, they need to think more critically, creatively, innovatively with the goal of finding lasting solutions to our perennial problems.

Eckhart Tolle wrote: "True intelligence operates silently. Stillness is where creativity and solutions to problems are found"

" Eckhart Tolle is a German-born resident of Canada, best known as the author of The Power of Now and A New Earth: Awakening to Your Life's Purpose. In 2011, he was listed by Watkins Review as the most spiritually influential person in the world." Source: Wikipedia

When I came back to Nigeria in 2005, almost everyone advised me to seek some kind of spiritual protection and guidance from the source of their choice. That was "what everyone does here", they said. I had been away from Nigeria for a long time. Could they be right?

Hmmmmm

Even though I did not have any belief system, and I still do not, I decided to "test" the effectiveness of these so called spiritual guidance/protection centres.

My first test was to find out if these spiritual people could "see". And, the first two "prophets" could not "see". One, on a fishing expedition, asked me where my mother was. I answered him that my mother was in Ojodu Lagos Nigeria. He said I should go and tell my mother to pray for me. If he could truly "see", he would have known that my mother was dead and was buried at Ojodu Lagos, Nigeria.The alfa and the babalawo I visited were just as "blind" as the first two "prophets". I could "see" clearer than all of them. So, logically, I now "see" for myself.

Even though a lot people may not see it as such. But the above is really about deficient cultural and religious leadership in this part of the world.

Where are those who could truly "see"? "Ti a ba de oju, a ri imu". If we squint in the direction of our nose, we will be able to see our nose.

Life does not do as it likes, meaning it is not capricious. Behind the apparent worldly chaos, there is order. There are natural laws that govern the universe. That knowledge is accessible to those who strive to access it.

Life is art and science combined. The science part is the fixed laws. The art part is what you do, creatively or otherwise, with the fixed part.

Nature has provided. But we must nurture. Nature is unkind to those who fail to nurture. Failure to nurture always leads to underdevelopment, to stagnation, then, to retrogression.
Make nurturing all your "hidden Human Resources" a priority in 2017.

The sole purpose of going to school is to get educated, not just to get a certificate. The certificate is just to confirm that one attended certain school. It is also to confirm that one finished from that school. However, we are all aware that it is possible for one to obtain a certificate without being properly educated.

Using the same analogy, the sole purpose of going to religious houses is to become spiritual, not just to become religious. The attendance at the religious houses is just to confirm that one is receiving instruction on how to become spiritual. However, we know it is possible to attend regular service at religious houses without becoming spiritual. I am using the word "spiritual" here to mean "going beyond the seen into the unseen for the sole purpose of obtaining spiritual guidance."

After graduating from school, one will naturally go into the world, in search of job. It is on the job that the adequacy, the effectiveness of one's education will be verified.

Same thing ought to apply to the one attending services at religious houses. Naturally, when he goes out to mingle in the world, his behavior ought to confirm the glorious instructions he has been consuming from his/her preferred religious house. Is he humble? Is he just? Is he loving? Is he successful? Is he happy? Is he upright, and therefore, not corrupt? Does he do the right things the right way even if no one is looking?

The final analysis is this: The quality of productivity and efficiency should be used in determining who is truly versed in the art of living. Fruits, ladies and gentlemen, fruits are the ultimate verification of what type a tree is.

Mental is the same as spiritual. It is also the same as psychological. While mental deals with the known, spiritual deals with the unknown.

Spiritual weakness manifests as mental weakness. Lack of creativity, innovation are manifested symptoms of this. Those that are mentally weak cannot produce anything mentally. And is it not true that those who cannot produce mentally also cannot produce products, services of modern convenience? Are you still wondering why our Naira is weak and continues to weaken?

Mental, spiritual weakness always leads to stagnation, retrogression, subjugation.

We were enslaved, colonized because of this simple fact. The fact that we have since "borrowed" strength from our enslavers. colonizer's have not strengthened us mentally, spiritually. A borrower is a perpetual servant to the lender.

Whenever we are ready, we must retrace our steps to our humble beginnings, recognize and repair our true mental, spiritual weakness, strengthen it, make it resistant to financial slavery and colonization that is looming with our ever slippery national Naira.

Faithfully defending weakness does not produce strength. Those who have lost the ability to tell the difference between truth and lies will forever be weak, forever ripe for enslavement, for colonization. Truth always depart from those who, because of selfishness, continue to defend delusion (false beliefs and outright lies) even when it is clear that they are wrong. Acceptance of truth is the antidote for delusion. It is a prerequisite for growth, for progress.

Nigeria is the way it is because of the way we were, because of the way we are. Let us change our thoughts and behavior if we want this country to change. Or...let us continue to enjoy it without change. I am cool with that. Cheers.

CHAPTER 8

WHAT IS MEDITATION?

Meditation is simply a breathing exercise with a focus on in and out breathing. Just like going to the gym helps to develop the muscles, meditation helps to develop sharpness of the mind. It is for those who want to develop their minds, their innate human resources. It is to clean, calm your mind and immersed it in better, pertinent knowledge. There is a part of our brain that meditation awakens. And that part provides guidance in doing the right things, the right way, in all things, and at all times.

I use meditation to train my mental muscles. And it has awakened me beyond my conditioned mind and habitual thinking. When my mind is calm, and silent, yet completely alert, I always experience a state of profound, deep peace.

I learned two types of meditation in 1996: choice-less awareness and directed awareness. In choice-less awareness, one simply sit in meditation, concentrating on one's breathing, and let whatever comes to come. But in directed awareness, one focuses on something in particular, like a vexing problem that needs to be solved, a concept in need of a deeper understanding etc.

Within one week of learning meditation, my inner life came alive. I began to see images in my meditation. And my intuition accelerated.

There are many different ways to practice meditation. The method I used most of the time is done this way:

I lie down on my bed. I cover my body with bed-sheet to avoid distractions. I relax all my muscles. I remove my awareness from my surrounding. I concentrate on my in and out breathing by counting from one to hundred. I lie there until my body begins to feel like I am sleeping. However, my mind is always alive underneath. This, I call "Trance state." I just stay there and wait for whatever might happen.

Sometimes I see images without understanding what they mean. Sometimes I understand what the images mean. Sometimes I let ideas, thoughts, and images roam freely through my mind with the hope that they may lead to some new solution to certain vexing problems. Sometimes I just lie there and enjoy the peace and calmness that come from within. Sometimes I experience a state of mystical awareness of "God's" being. Sometimes I learn more about myself. Sometimes I see familiar things in a different way. Sometimes I acquire new knowledge. Sometimes I catch a glimpse of the past and the future. Sometimes the understanding of my dreams comes to me. All the time I hear the voice. Sometimes I try not to think of anything and just blank out my mind with no conscious awareness.

Meditation, like I have said, is a breathing exercise. It is to the mind what the gym is to the body. Those who spend quality time cultivating their mind will get fulfilling moments harvesting its output. What can a man do without his mind? Is the mind not the tool used in perceiving, believing, deciding? A malfunctioning mind will ruin the life of its possessor. And a beautiful mind will not only produce success and happiness for its possessor, it will also produce contentment. You are still wondering why you should master meditation? I recommend that you learn and practice meditation.

The same year I learned meditation, 1996, I was in deep meditation, praying--yes, praying. I used to pray then--for knowledge, wisdom, and understanding. After the customary calmness and stillness of mind that meditation induces, I silently "heard"--or was it "know"?--"Go through the same channel." Go through the same channel how? I thought I could pray and get knowledge, wisdom, and understanding from a dream. I thought wrong.

In that same 1996, I was in meditation. And I felt that I was going deeper than before. Then, I suddenly began to feel a sense of apprehension that bordered on fear. Why should I be afraid to go deeper into myself? Intuition spoke silently again: "Go and learn what is known and come back for what is unknown."

Okay. That was when my appetite for knowledge got bigger and my thirst for knowledge increased. I began to spend most of my waking time in the library, soaking in what was known in preparation to go back inward for what was unknown. These are the things that have to be acquired through conscious, continuous striving.

By the end of 1996, a silent voice surfaced in my meditation and fully took over the teaching that is still going on up until today.

One of the objectives of meditation is to stop thinking, to go beyond thinking and rely on intuition. It may take longer than you think to achieve result in your meditation. Sometimes it does. But you must resist taking short cuts. With patience, constant practice, you will ultimately achieve excellent results.

A lot of people have not been taught how to think. They have been taught what to think. And they simply recall those information and they think they are thinking. Meditation will help you to clear the debris of your mind by melting what others have taught you to think, to believe, and you will begin to think, creatively, innovatively, positively, for yourself.

One of the goals of meditation is to develop power of the mind. Those who have power of the mind can manifest that power by the productions of their minds. Effective living, cell phones, good systems, airplanes, ships, televisions are few examples of productions of the mind. And those with weakness of the mind can also manifest that weakness by the production of their minds. Ineffective living, stories of past performances and old glories, more stories of un-provable subjects, delusion are few example of weakness of the mind. I have move beyond stories, to the development of the power of mind. I am tired of telling "prove-less" stories.

Drones are weapons of war, a manifestation of the Europeans' technological advancement. The operator of the drone merely sits in an air-conditioned room, far away from harm's way, sipping coffee, smoking a cigarette, using joystick to remote controlled unmanned plane that targets and bombs suspected terrorists/enemies.

And what do we have as manifestations of our "un-technological advancement"? Some people sending "holy ghost fire" to kill their enemies and others, tagging natural, preventable, treatable ailments as "spiritual attacks" from the enemy.

Still others get bombed by Boko Haram and do nothing, hoping that their self-defence is not in their hands but in "God's" hands.

To bridge this technological gap, our minds must evolve creatively. Or else... they will continue to make aircrafts while we will continue to make witchcrafts. Both are some form of craft. Not so?

Everyone has muscles. But not everyone is "cut up". Those with finely chiselled body, bulging biceps, flat tummy, have invested time in the gym, on the tracks, to arrive at that destination. They eat balanced diet that complement their rigorous workouts. It is neither by juju/charm, nor by prayer. They simply followed a disciplined workout regimen. They nurtured what nature had provided for them.

The same analogy can be applied to the human mind. Everyone has a mind. Not so? I am now assuming that the mind houses the human intelligence. Therefore, the mind is akin to the control center, the determinant factor for the effective utilization of all the other human resources/talents. Without a sound mind, no matter how strong the body is, the chance of becoming a load carrier at Oyingbo Market increases, the chance of being poor, high. The mind is the tool for acquiring knowledge, wisdom, and understanding. And these come through focused, disciplined study, observation, experimentation, verification, experience, intuition, creative thinking. Did you hear me mention juju/ charm/praying? Ok, you did not. That is because leading countries of the world use the former formula and not the latter.

And anyone interested in excellence, in leading, in living a fulfilling life devoid of problems, must learn how to do the right things the right way, in all things, and at all times. Nature/Providence/"God" has provided the raw materials. Failure to develop, refine those raw materials is the essence of stagnation, subjugation.

Like I said, Nature/"God" has already provided all the materials (input) we need to be successful, to be happy, and to continually add value to our society. However, we need to master the ways and means (process) to turn these provided materials into desirable, favorable lives/products (output). Potential is not actual. But potential can be transformed to actual with the mastery of the input-process-output model.

Truth and delusion, unfortunately, spring from the same source. It is through verification, experience we can separate one from the other. We must be cautious when we think abstractly. We must protect our mental health by installing verifying "devices" inside our head. I know this because my mind used to lie to me a lot. It still does, but less and less. It would manufacture opinions that were wrong. It would make me believe things that were not truthful. And it would deceive me and made me accept other people's assumptions, superstitions, without verification. But when I learned how to meditate, just the breathing exercise, it cleared my mind of most of its debris. It melted away most of my erroneous opinions, assumptions, and superstitions. It allowed me to know that I did not know as much as I thought I knew. It birthed my curiosity, ignited my passion to learn, to know. Consequently, it transported me to the psychological territory where intuition accelerated. That was when I discovered the importance of doing the right things the right way, in all things, and at all times. And creativity, the replacing of old lifestyle with a new and better, more satisfying, more fulfilling one ensued. And happiness gushed, love bloomed.

Do you have a need for self-respect, strength, competence, mastery, self-confidence, independence, and freedom? Then meditation is for you. You can use meditation to develop the inner competence derived from experience. Practicing meditation requires no change in beliefs or lifestyle.

No matter what station you are, if as at today, you do not feel fulfilled, if you are mostly unhappy, you are doing some things wrong. Happiness is a by-product of fulfilling activities. And everyone, I repeat, everyone has the human ability to be happy. It is those simple choices we routinely make that are responsible for either our happiness or our pain

I see people, a lot of people, struggling to put a 20kg load on a stand designed to carry a 10kg load. Of course they are not stupid people. They are only trying to follow the dictates of their religion, of their culture.

As for me, I neither struggle, nor suffer. I simply put a 10kg load on a stand designed to carry a 10kg load. As a mystical creative rebel, I stay afloat, even in troubling times. I live, love, laugh, without religious, cultural encumbrance.

CHAPTER 9

CONSCIOUS AND UNCONSCIOUS IGNORANCE

Most people read books, understand what they have read, and repeat it. In doing so, are using the lowest level of intelligence to accomplish that.

However, there is a higher level of intelligence usage. This level of higher intelligence usage synthesizes information from different sources. It then converts it into useful, practical knowledge. And the fruits of that knowledge are always delicious to people, countries that possess the knowledge. They will produce. And they will progress.

We have not even started our own collective organic mental growth towards enlightenment. Can we not tell a tree by the fruits it bears? Meditation is a catalyst in organic mental growth. I have tested it, tasted it, and found it to be delicious indeed.

Some people do not know. Yet, they are unaware that they do not know. Maybe they have simply used up their learning capabilities. They will simply form uninformed opinions and splash the world with ignorance. I usually dodge my head from such splashing. Sometimes the splashing of the world with ignorance is a derivative of wrong knowledge or archaic beliefs.

However, some people do not know. And they are aware that they do not know. So, with the awareness of their ignorant status, they will use that ignorance to ask questions, to learn, and become enlightened, in order to live orderly life that is symptomatic of enlightened souls. May the "God of Truth" always allow me to pitch my tent in the camp of the latter group.

I read this "Ancient Prayer" sometimes in 1996 and I find it pertinent to this chapter:

Ancient Prayer.
"From the cowardice that shrinks
From new truths
From the laziness that is content
With half-truths
From the arrogance that thinks
It knows all the truths
O God of Truth, deliver us."

Thinking is the essence of everything created by humans. Thinking can be classified as useful or useless, valuable or valueless, creative or destructive, old or new, ethical or unethical. Thinking that is new and useful, that is creative and valuable, and that is ethical and legal, ultimately create new values for the individual, for the society. A continually new-values-creating society is a less corrupt one.

Take a mental audit today. Is your thinking creating new values for yourself and your society? Or is it merely a repetition of the same old thinking that has gotten us nowhere favourable, nor desirable? Can you or anyone honestly say his/her life has gotten better because of your thinking?

The gate of change is within each individual. And only that individual can fling that door open. So if any segment of your thinking is the opposite of those mentioned above, it is time to commence the changing process. We must create the type of society that we, and our lineage, can live in comfortably, and be proud of ultimately.

I know that everyone wants to be successful and happy. But we have to develop the required basic mental skills to achieve success and happiness. The happiness of our lives depends upon the quality of our thoughts. And, like I keep on saying, we can enhance the quality of our thoughts through critical thinking, through meditation.

We have to develop the ability to focus for long period of time, a propensity for balanced and critical thinking, and a knack for quietly empowering others. These basic mental skills, which include concentration, goal-setting, imagery and mental rehearsal, relaxation and self-talk are imperative for anyone who wants lasting success and enduring happiness.

We should not be like some dangerous people that have made some mistakes, that are making some mistakes, yet, are not aware that they have made the mistakes, that they are making some mistakes. Instead, they blame others, witches and wizards for their misfortunes, which are consequences of their mistakes. Some mistakes, if not most, are truly consequences of erroneous thinking, bad choices, and ineffective decisions.

With meditation, we can observe our thoughts as they arise in our mind. With critical thinking skills, we can analyse the consequences of our actions before we act. A well-knitted lifestyle must be planned and not just hoped for. Proper planning is known to prevent poor performance. Be wise

For every right we have as humans, there is an obligation attached to it. In order to continue to enjoy any right, we must continue to fulfill the obligation attached to it. So, if it is true that the prayers of those who do not follow the law is abomination in the eyes of "God", then following the law is an obligation that must be fulfilled by those of us who want our prayers answered. "God" is not deaf. It is as simple as that. We must "do the right things, the right way, in all things, at all times, without hypocrisy. Praying, without doing the right things, therefore, is an exercise in futility, a mere wishful thinking that confers no clear advantage. It was true in antiquity that faith without work is dead. It is still true in modern times that we must work towards whatever we want as individuals, as a nation.

Do we want a lawful, peaceful, progressive nation? We must become those things we want. Those who come to equity, it was said, must come with clean hands. Oya, abeg, go and clean your hands jor. Then come back to equity. No be only government people hands dirty fa.

One of the tests of leadership is the ability to recognize a problem before it becomes an emergency. ---Arnold H. Glasow. And, a lot of problems can be prevented from the point of decision making.

Also, a lot of problems can be prevented during the thought process.

Henceforth, before making any decision--no exception--think well, think critically, think creatively, analyse the facts. Teach your children to do the same. It is dangerous not to teach our children how to think critically for themselves and how to analyze facts.

It is true that those simple choices we routinely make are responsible for either our happiness or our pain To lessen our pain and increase our joy, we need to learn how to make better, more effective choices. Tighten your thoughts with the aid of meditation, competent research and verification. We need more critical, creative, innovative thinkers in this nation. Prevention, it has been said, is better than cure.

Learn meditation and practice it routinely. Apart from it being the tool to tap into our unconscious mind, it keeps you balanced, keep you focused on doing the things that will ultimately lead to enduring happiness and lasting success. It is your life. And the decision is yours. Choose wisely.

We have been taught how to be powerless, how to seek solution from external factors instead of from within. And we have learned well. We are even teaching the next generation how to do as we do.

Hmmmmm......

While acting in our powerless capacity, we powerlessly look on at our currency's steady decline. Some of us fold our arms. And some raise their hands to the sky seeking divine intervention. But, still, the Naira continues to decline.
It is time to unlearn how to be powerless. It is time to learn how to be empowered from within by awakening the sleeping giant within us. Do you feel you have a giant within you that can be awakened?

Just like I have said earlier, to learn and understand, to analyze what has been understood, requires the usage of lower level of intelligence. And most people function on this level. To cope with new, trying situation, to synthesize, requires the usage of higher level of intelligence. Only few people have managed to grasp this. It is from synthesis, from "the combining of the constituent elements of separate material or abstract entities into a single or unified entity" that new thoughts are formed, created, discovered, and not from analysis, from mindless repetition of what has been committed to books. It is from synthesizing that new intellectual value, production, is achieved.

No "God" has restricted me from using the higher level intelligence to cope with new, trying situation, no "God". "God" is not deaf. That is why I do not conform to what has been committed to books but to continually pursue new, effective methods of problem solving.

"A danger of idealism is being caught on the mental plane. Lofty thoughts and talks are never enough; the one who would taste success must eventually enter the world of practice." Ideals are good but practicality is what matter most. "We are what we repeatedly do..." Don't just tell me. Show me. And make a believer out of me. Your decision decides your direction. And your direction decides your destination. Decide well so you can arrive at a desirable and favorable destination. That, ladies and gentlemen, is success.

Why is it that we never developed our own ideology in modern time? Why do we always import ideology when we can simply produce our own? Is it because we do not know how to produce common thoughts? Or is it that our higher level use of intelligence is defective, thereby preventing us from synthesizing information?

Ideology is defined as "a systematic body of concepts especially about human life or culture..." Ideology is a commodity. It can either be produced, refined, locally, or it can be imported. Some people even have fancy name for it. Some called it religion, with different brand names, while some called it a way of life. Water is simply water no matter where you put it. And, a rose flower, called by any name, will still smell the same way to those who know what a rose flower smell like. Not so?

Ideology is a commodity. We need to create our own. That is one of the functions of that thing we call brain. We need to stop this shameless importation of what we can produce. We are no longer under colonization. It is okay to think for ourselves now. Let us define our own reality ourselves, for ourselves. Let us move away from "cut and paste" leaders. Maybe we too can start exporting ideology, instead of importing it, after we have mastered its production. Let us strengthen our Naira by strengthening our collective brain. Even though we have our own, crude, (pun intended) crying for astute brain to refine it, we keep clinging to that of others, claiming they are the best. We were bred to consume the finest but not to produce it.

Ideology is a commodity in the global marketplace. And, every commodity requires a sales-force. We have to become salespeople for our own ideology. Why import what we can produce? Why import if we can produce?

I of course no longer import those things that I can produce. Names are among those things that I can produce. And, ideas about "God" too.

The value of the Naira is tied to our production as a people and our consumptive habits. We just have to produce to strengthen it. There is no shortcut to strengthening the Naira. Every time we buy a foreign product, value leaves Nigeria and is added to the country from which that product originates.

When we are ignorant, and we are not aware that we are ignorant, we tend to suffer unnecessarily. There is a correlation between ignorance and suffering. I am very certain that ignorance is a factor in most human suffering.

Listen to this story that showcases ignorance and suffering. I sent someone to buy coffee, sugar, powdered milk for me. He has performed that chore for me many times before. I gave him 3000 Naira. Nescafé coffee is about 600 Naira. Dangote sugar is about

500 Naira. And, Peak powdered milk is about 1000 Naira. His transport fare is 200 Naira. All came to 2,300 Naira. He was supposed to bring 700 Naira change.

Before he left, I transferred 500 Naira Etisalat credit to his phone so that he could call me if he needed to. Guess what? After I had done what was required to make his job go smoothly, the man introduced stupidity into the game. And he ended up suffering by walking home, sweating profusely.

Here was what happened: The Adidde store he went to did not have Peak powdered milk. And instead of calling to tell me, he chose to unilaterally act stupid by buying a different brand of powdered milk, which was about double the price of Peak powdered milk, which, I do not like the taste.

His ignorance affected me only in a small way. But it made him to suffer by walking back when he could have come back in comfort. The good thing is. "oni iya ni o ma je eyi ti o po ju ninu iya re"? It is the owner of the suffering that will enjoy more from his/her suffering. It is indeed true that those simple choices we routinely make are responsible for either our happiness or our pain

CHAPTER 10

OF THOUGHTS AND SIGHT

It is very possible to have sight, to look, and not see. And it is very possible to look, but instead of seeing what is in front of us, we see our prejudice, the stereotype that has been pounded into us from birth. Therefore, we fail to see reality as it is. We see it as we are. We see it as we have been conditioned to see it.

However, we can learn how to look and see what is in front of us without seeking succour in prejudices and stereotypes. And, once we have learned how to see clearly, and ultimately, how to think clearly and accurately, disappointment will depart from us. Frustration will flee! Clarity will come. Then, effective decision-making comes naturally. And, ultimately, tribal and religious bigotry will be mitigated.

Frustration is "the feeling of being upset or annoyed as a result of being unable to change or achieve something." It is a relative of anger and disappointment.

If the feelings of frustration, dissatisfaction, dejection are not enough to tell us that things are not working well, nothing else may be able to tell us. A clear understanding of how reality truly works is an antidote to frustration.

The level of our frustration, dissatisfaction is proportional to the level of our true knowledge. Counting the tail of a dog as a leg will not increase the dog's legs to five. Fortunately, the level of our inner peace, joy is also proportional to our true knowledge.

Those who consistently get what they expected to get always bubble with nice feelings, recession or no recession, inflation or no inflation.

Just imagine that, prior to the 2015 presidential election, I "heard" " Muhammadu Buhari will win" from my mental / spiritual / psychological realm. And because I had no prejudicial, stereotypical thoughts that would cloud what I "heard", I heeded the inner message and aligned my actions in its direction.

When reality finally hit home, and the announcement that GMB had won the election was pronounced by Prof. Athairu Jega, I felt no disappointment, no frustration, and consequently, no anger, no negative emotions. I only had a sense of accomplishment, of fulfillment. My thinking that I no longer suffered from cognitive dissonance was reinforced. I continued to live, to love, to laugh, sans celebration. Now, tell me quick, who is saved and who is not?

I have discovered that I learn new things through three different methods. The first method is learning from someone else which includes learning from books. The second method is learning from, ah, that harsh teacher called experience. The third method is via natural knowing. Call it intuition if you like.

However, to know that I know, (I use beliefs sparingly) I usually combine at least two of the three methods mentioned above. Gradually but surely, I am working towards my own "salvation", which means, to me, the liberation of me from my ignorance, from my delusion.

In my opinion, the universe is very complex. There are multiple truths. Some truths that appear to be "absolute" to some people may not even apply to others. We ought to find our own truths in our own experiences. We must begin to Define Our Own Reality.

What we called "truths", are they working for us? Do they produce love, laughter, peace of mind? Do they produce favourable and desirable outcomes?

Truth always works, if not in the interim, in the long run. And if we have found our own "truths", we should not impose them on others. Limiting others to our own limitations is a cause of war all over the world.

I have found my own set of "truths". That is why I continue to live, love, laugh. I hope you have found yours. Or I hope you eventually will. I have defined my own reality. Go ahead and define yours.

As a nation, we must go back to the drawing board with a new set of leaders that can mentally, spiritually "see". Quality mind produces quality thinking. Quality thinking produces quality leaders. Quality leaders produce quality culture. Quality culture produces quality minds, quality followers. And quality followers nourish a nation. Then, quality nation produces good quality of life for all.

Why are we not getting it right? First of all, most of our institutions are imported. Second of all, corruption and incompetence are embedded in them, turning them into, imitations of the real thing. Consequently, we have bad institutions, one of the prerequisite of poor countries and, the main reason why we continue to wobble.

Dissatisfaction is a symptom of paying for an original item but given a fake instead. Disappointment is a symptom of expecting an original item but getting a fake one. Satisfaction is a symptom of knowing what you are buying and getting exactly what you have bought.

Nigeria is the way it is because of who we are. The script we are acting on, we did not write. Most of our best actors are acting from foreign scripts, from borrowed scripts. The poor is corrupt because of what to eat. The rich is corrupt because of greed. Dissatisfaction and Disappointment are now in abundant supply. Those who are truly satisfied are in the minority.

We must not just fold our hands and wait for "God" to do all the work. While we endure the endurable, with endurance, we ought to be changing the changeable, with accurate vision, with courage, and enjoying the enjoyable, with laughter, with love. Since all things are created twice, the mental creation should proceed immediately. The physical creation can either proceed simultaneously, depending on our level of mental growth, or it should proceed sooner than later.

The following questions are meant to help us reposition and realign ourselves to the true yearnings of our heart:

(1)   Do you think there are more you can accomplish in life and will like to know more about yourself and your innate human potentials?

(2)   Do you desire inner peace and joy but the hustle and bustle of daily living is preventing you from achieving this?

(3)   Are you stuck in the rut and will like to start moving upward the ladder of success?

(4)   Are you always short of disposable income and will like to develop "cut your coat according to your fabrics" skills without sacrificing your happiness?

(5)   Will you like to develop your creative and innovative
        abilities?

If your answer to any of these questions is yes, creating your own
ideology may be for you.

"If you wish to move mountains tomorrow, you must start by
lifting stones today." -African Proverb

Ideology is a commodity. And you can create your own. That is
one of the functions of that thing we call brain. Let us stop this
shameless importation of what we can produce. We are no longer
under colonization. It is okay to think for ourselves now. Let us
define our own reality ourselves, for ourselves by moving away
from "cut and paste" leaders. Maybe we too can start exporting
ideology, instead of importing it, after we have mastered its
production. Let us strengthen our Naira by strengthening our
collective brain. "When a storm is coming, all other birds seek
shelter. The eagle alone avoids the storm by flying above it."

Do you have the wherewithal to fly above the storm? I have met
people that are naturally intelligent, yet whose beliefs limit their
thoughts. And consequently, they could not grow intellectually,
mentally, beyond those beliefs. Did I just describe one of the
recipes of stagnation?

CHAPTER 11

ERUPTION OF CONTENTMENT

About seventeen years ago, year 2000 to be precise, it dawned on me that I did not need as much as I thought I needed to be happy, to be satisfied. That was the day that most things became well with me. With, or without a lot of things, I now feel complete, happy, satisfied.

If those things come my way, fine. If they don't, fine. My equanimity will not be disturbed by my lack of certain things. Life is good, not because I have all that I want, but because I am content with what I have. That means I always cut my coat according to my fabrics.

I do not envy anyone. I never had, and hopefully, I never will envy anyone. Some things that others have, I may not have. And that is okay. That is life. We all cannot have the same things. But some things I do have, others do not have also. Again, that's okay. That's life. We all cannot have the same things. I have love, plenty of it. I am always bubbling with inner peace, inner joy. I live. I laugh. And I am content with the things I have. I sow. I reap. I strictly adhere to the immutable law of cause and effect. And I do not covet my neighbors' things.

So, I advise you to live, love, laugh, and enjoy the simple pleasures that life has to offer. Life is good, but you must plan it well.

I have thrown all my frustrations into the burning furnace of contentment. I have gotten rid of grudges. Grudge is a persistent feeling of ill will or resentment resulting from a past insult. I have gotten rid of malice. Malice is the desire to harm someone; ill will.

I have gotten rid of hatred. Hatred is intense dislike; hate. I have gotten rid of greed. Greed is intense and selfish desire for something, especially wealth, power, or food. And, contentment has erupted. Contentment is a state of happiness and satisfaction.

My contentment is not the fulfillment of all that I want, but it is the realization of how much I already have. True contentment is when our happiness comes from what we have, unattached to what we do not have.

Sometimes in 2015, I was driving from Lagos State into Ogun State. The ride was smooth. I was cruising. Wow. Beautiful. The K-1 Ultimate's music blaring from the car stereo was exhilarating. That customary nice feeling came. The one that is attached to the enjoyment of simple pleasures of life. I smiled. Then, for an unexplained reason, the thought of my first grandson, Meziah, flashed through my mind. And pure pleasure rose from somewhere within me. And it spread all over my entire body. It was then I said to myself: "This is heaven".

It would be pure greed to want more joy. Life is good. But it must be planned well. I still feel the same way I felt that day, two years ago, recession or no recession.

Sometimes, the old must be dismantled before the new can be built. In my own case, I had to dismantle my profligate lifestyle in order to erect a new, simple lifestyle where I cut my coat according to my fabrics, where contentment reigns as King. Here, I am using the word "profligate" in all its dictionary meaning.
Now....

While some people are hurting,
I am healing.
While some are hating,
I'm loving.

While others are complaining about life,
I am content, enjoying simple solitude, simple pleasures of life.
Tell me quick,
Am I not among Fortune's favorite children?
Of course I am.

The truly guided, whether secular or spiritual, live an orderly life
and not one in disarray. They live a contented life and not one of
perpetual lacking, not one of unending dissatisfaction. There is
nothing beyond satisfaction but greed. Those who always need
more to be satisfied when less can also be satisfying ought to
check their greed level. It may be high.

CHAPTER 12

AWAKE THE SLEEPING GIANT WITHIN YOU

Some are willing but unable.
Some are able but unwilling.
Still, some are willing and able.
Ah! It is only those that are willing, that are able, will get "it".

Nature/"God" has already provided all the materials (input) we need to be successful, to be happy, and to continually add value to our society.

However, we need to master ways and means (process) to turn these provided materials into desirable, favorable lives/products/services(output).

Potential is not actual. But potential can be transformed into actual with the mastery of the input-process-output model. It is our duty and no one else to learn how to empower ourselves and break the chain of learned helplessness and generational classical conditioning.

In order to do this, we need power. What is power? It is simply the ability to achieve. What can we do without power? Mostly, nothing. Therefore understanding power is absolutely necessary.

These are the types of power formulated by social psychologists John R. P. French and Bertram Raven in 1959 and 1965.

(1)   Legitimate power.
(2)   Reward power.
(3)   Expert power.
(4)   Referent power.

(5)   Coercive power.
(6)   Informational power.

Legitimate power is formal power. For example, if we see a policeman with a gun, we know that he has the formal power to carry the gun because he represents authority and, therefore, authorized to carry arms.

Reward power is the ability to reward anyone who has done something for us.

Expert power is when we possess the knowledge and skills to get some things done effectively.

Referent Power is the charismatic ability to inspire followers to be loyal and emulate the person that possesses it

Coercive power is to be able to force others to do what we want them to do even if they do not want to do it.

Information power is to possess timely, accurate, and pertinent information.

To achieve any objective or goal in life, we need the right combination of powers. Without the right combination, we may suffer from "illusion of power", and achievement of objectives/goals may be elusive. And, those without appropriate types of power blame external factors for their woes. They may even believe that their family is cursed.

Anyone who believes he/she is suffering from "ogun idile", generational curse, is actually suffering from generational ignorance, and in need of total psychological formatting. Meditation, as a tool, will format our mind by cleansing it of all its debris, its delusion. And it will awake the sleeping giant within us.

But we must be self-disciplined, self-controlled, so the awakened giant will not trample on the rights of others. One of the benefits of meditation is a peaceful and contented mind.

What is Meditation? Meditation is a training of mental attention that awakens us beyond the conditioned mind and habitual thinking, and reveals the nature of reality. It trains the mind to focus on the in and out breathing while cutting off the internal dialogue (Cessation of thoughts).

Anyone that thinks his or her problems are caused by "aye", witches, wizards, needs to go and do his/her "shadow" work. "The Shadow" is a psychological concept formulated by Carl Jung. I find it pertinent, useful.

Most of the time, the problem is "within". And our intelligence, with its intuitive component firing, can assist in, not only solving problems, but also in pre-empting and preventing problems.

Intelligence is not just the ability to learn and understand. It is also the ability to cope with new and trying situations. Take that for what it is. The usage of higher level of intelligence can be an antidote to the prevention, and resolution of most problems.

Anyone that consistently lacks money needs to look inward and resolve the problem that is creating the lack. Stop for a minute. Look around you. See those poor, old miserable people? Yes, they were once young, like us, and full of life, full of hopes. They once believed, in "God", and in themselves. Yet they still ended up, in their old age, poor, miserable, and sometimes loveless.

What went wrong? At some point in their lives, they made life-ruining mistakes. And they eventually stopped learning, stopped growing.

And some of us are, unconsciously, making the same life-ruining mistakes. We have stopped learning, stopped growing. We need to become conscious of these mistakes, and we need to correct them before it is too late.

Through meditation, we can develop the power of our mind so we can make effective decisions that will prevent making life-ruining mistakes.

Meditation differs from prayer in that it is primarily an orientation of the mind. It brings about realizations and recognitions which become formulated knowledge. It is our life. It is our choice. Let us choose wisely.

That day in year 1996 when I discovered that I was reaping what I sowed, that I always reap what I sow, was a very important day in my life. That was the day I began creating my own thoughts, the day I became free to do as I please, as long as I do no harm to others.

This year, 2017 when this book is written, makes it seventeen years of uninterrupted peace and joy. And, my uninterrupted peace and joy are the by-products of striving to do the right things the right way.

My life experience, my thoughts, my actions are now in alignment, in sync. Life simply throws back at me what I throw at it, big or small, good or bad.

Like the fabled Phoenix, I have risen from the ashes of my failure. Those who knew me seventeen years ago will understand exactly what I am saying.

Simply put, I have found me. The giant in me is awake. And, I have found my purpose in life.

CHAPTER 13

DEFINING MY OWN REALITY

When I first started hearing the "voice" inside my head in 1996, my younger brother, Niyi, was one of the few people I told. And he said, without verification, "Ah! That's our mother's voice you are hearing. "

Imagine that. He was wrong, of course. I was actually hearing a silent, male "voice." I was in an uncharted psychological landscape, unknown to my younger brother, unknown to many.

With time, with verification, and of course with experience, I knew the "voice" I was hearing inside my head. I was definitely

hearing the voice of reasoning. I was probably hearing the voice of "God". I was hearing a "voice" that constantly compelled me to do the right things the right way, in all things and at all times. I was hearing a "voice" that constantly guided me up to the point where nothing negative going in Nigeria affects me negatively.

Presently, I always wake up every morning, with a smile, with the feeling that I do not need anything. And that feeling is not because I have everything, because I do not. But I am content with what I have. I crave for nothing anymore. I feel fulfilled, despite the state of affairs in Nigeria. I feel satisfied, even though there is recession in the land, coupled with a biting inflation that is making the price of essential commodities skyrocketing. I feel so complete albeit I have been unable to have all my children under one roof. I feel peace inside me, around me. I have love in my heart, in my life.

If I never have more than this in life, I will still die smiling, laughing, knowing that I have lived a fulfilled life, with a feeling of completeness. The juice of joy inside my belly is enough for an elephant to dance the jig.

I now live in a self-created cocoon. In my cocoon, there is joy. There is love. And there is peace. There is no undue financial burden in my cocoon.
I have mastered the art of living within the confine of my meagre means.

Anyone bringing strife and discord and problems is not welcome in my cocoon. Anyone bringing undue financial burden born out of penchant for extraneous appetites is definitely not welcome.

In my cocoon, there is always light, light in all its meaning. And there is this marvellous contentment born out of jettisoning of extraneous appetites.

In my cocoon, I get the same feeling you get from jetting out of Lagos after dinner, having breakfast and shopping in Dubai, then proceeding to America to party with family and friends.

Simply put, I have mastered the art of enjoying the simplest pleasures that life has to offer. I have heard some people calling this luck. Hmmmm, luck ko, luck ni. This is the result of many years of prudent planning, of rearrangement of thoughts and priorities, of washing my hands clean of all illegality and corruption. Now, I live in my cocoon, with clean hands, without rancor, without malice, laughing, loving, living.

My contentment is not unconnected with my conviction that I have always, and I will always, reap what I sow, good or bad, big or small. I pity those who do not reap what they sow. That, in my opinion, is akin to someone working for months without getting paid.

My ability to deal with adversity with equanimity is also not
unconnected with my conviction of sowing and reaping. If I am
reaping a sour harvest as a consequence of bad sowing, why
waver, why wobble? Why not just calmly adjust the thinking, the
doing that preceded the bad sowing?

The following story showcases the above concepts. A close friend
from London sent a message to me through my aunty. As I was about
to drive out, to go and pick up the message, one of my house guests
came running out to stop me. She wanted
me to transfer MTN credit to her son. Her bank mobile apps was
misbehaving.

I did the transfer and she gave me the cash. She then apologized
for delaying me. I told her there was no reason to apologize, that
the way things have been working in my life, that she may have
saved me from sitting inside that menacing Lagos traffic.

Her daughter and son-in-law were witnessing all this. And I
explained the concept of synchronicity to all of them.
"Synchronicity is a concept, first explained by psychoanalyst Carl
Jung, which holds that events are "meaningful coincidences" if
they occur with no causal relationship yet seem to be
meaningfully related." Wikipedia.

As I was about to get in my car, I saw my cook coming out from the
back of the house. Wow! I instantly remembered that I had forgotten
to take with me the food I asked her to make for me. I knew that there
was no food where I was going. And I did not want to eat outside.

I went back in to tell my house guests what I would have forgotten
to take with me if someone had not ran out to "disturb" my initial
exit from the house. That is how synchronicity works for me.
Things I could not have done on my own get done by providence,

if I truly deserve them, if that is what my hand calls for, big or small, good or bad.

This was what killed my impatience, my frustration, and my disappointment. This is where my peace of mind, my joy springs from. I think what synchronicity is to me is what "grace" is to religious people. Those who feel it, not just believe it, know it.

This is the reason why I must not, I cannot depart from the path of continually striving to do the right things the right way, if not in all things, in most things, if not at all times, most of the time.

I like the idea of tithes. And I do pay tithes. But I pay it to neither a church, nor a pastor. I pay it into a special account I created for that purpose. This tithes is not money to be spent. It is strictly an emergency fund. It is an antidote for not going around begging mere mortals for rescue operations. It is also for me not to disturb "God" by ceaselessly asking for interventions. After all, "He" has endowed me with dominance over most things. Honestly, I think the world will be a lot "cleaner" if everyone "sweeps" his/her front and back yards. You don't have a "broom"? Get one! You do have a "broom", go ahead and "sweep"! Show me your bigger "broom" by how "clean/cleaner" your front/back yard is.

I bought my first car in 1981. And, since then, I have never changed any car tire myself. Therefore, up until today, I neither have the knowledge, nor the experience of changing car tires.

You may come to a conclusion, based on the above assertion, that I have never had a flat tire in my life. But that is not true. I have had several. But, funny enough, anytime I had a flat tire, there was always a vulcanizer nearby.

However, I remember one time, my friend and I were coming from Ekiti in 2010 and we had a flat tire. Alas, there was no vulcanizer in site. My friend changed the tire, sweating profusely.

I remembered telling him that he must have been doing some things wrong because I had never experience, on my own, what I experienced with him.

Fast forward to a November 2016 night in Ibadan. The same friend and another friend of mine, and I were at a meeting. During our conversation, I repeated it to them that I had never changed a flat tire in my life because anytime I had a flat, a vulcanizer was always around the corner.

That other friend and I left Ibadan for Lagos two days later. Shortly after getting on the expressway, one of our tires burst. And I calmly parked in front of the vulcanizer the universe has conspired to put in my path.

Was this luck, destiny, reaping what I sowed, coincidence, synchronicity or what? It is definitely not "answered prayer" because I stopped praying in 2000.

And witches and wizards had no hands in the tire that burst. That was a simple case of "anything that can go wrong will go wrong" if nothing is done to prevent it from going wrong. We could have prevented the burst time if we had heeded a caveat that the tire needed to be changed. Prevention is better than cure.

At the beginning of 2016, my water pumping machine went first. The plumber said it was our erratic electric supply that burned the coil. Then, the inverter followed. It blew up. My room's air conditioner decided to join the conspiracy to make me uncomfortable so I could start thinking of relocating to a foreign land. It simply stopped working despite it being connected to a stabilizer. The 42' plasma television too joined the bandwagon.

Can you imagine?

But....

The freezer remained loyal. "Won ti ni ko le buru titi ko ma ku enikan mo ni lara." It has been said that no matter how bad the situation is, at least one person will remain loyal. And it foiled the conspiracy to make me check out of here. Mi o lo si ibi kankan. ! I am not traveling anywhere, not anymore. It is inside this Nigeria I will continue to live and die.

Ah! Abi na witches and wizards from my village dey pursue me ni? Witches ko, wizards ni.

Again, the above episode simply highlighted one of my guiding principles that says,"anything that can go wrong will go wrong."

And now that it has gone wrong, then what?
Remember that 10% of my income that I told you I keep in a special account to assist "God" in assisting me in situation like this? The one that would not let me go, pan in hand, begging another mortal for assistance, because "God" is my strength? The exact same 10% that some people give to "men of God" as "God's" share of their income?

Yes, that was the account I dipped into to restore me back to my comfort zone. 2016 was my year of restoration.

It is not what is done to us, or what happens to us that hurts us. It is simply how we respond to what is done to us, or what happens to us, that hurts us. How we feel on the long run depends on our prior and present choices. Be aware. And choose wisely.

"God", the Higher Being, as we were taught, is omnipresent, omniscient. That means He is present everywhere. So, there is no need to call" Him" to come. And no one has the power to banish "Him" from anywhere. Not so?

That also means "He" knows all things. So, there is no need to tell him anything before" He" knows. And obviously it is impossible to lie to someone who already knows. Right? So, if you are present while your friend is choking, will you have to wait for him to make a request for assistance? If you have to, the world already has a word, or words, to describe you and your action.

Or imagine a policeman on patrol in civilized countries, (may not be applicable to Nigeria) who witnesses a crime but refuses to act because he was not summoned. What's that called?

The above reasoning is the reason why there is no need for me to pray again. I simply strive to do the right things the right way, in all things and at all times.
And is it not written somewhere that the prayer of those that do not follow the law is abomination in the eyes of "God"?

Okay, you think I am wrong for not praying and you are right for doing so? Please tell me quick: what is it you are getting from your prayer that I am not getting by not doing so? Make your answer something we can both experience, and not something restricted to your imagination.

As a mystic who draws directly from the "Source", dogmas and doctrines are not for me. "It is only those that are sick who need physician." May I continue to reap what I sow.

In 1997, I realized that a lot of my opinions were wrong. So, the overhauling of my mental landscape became imperative. The collapsing of my belief system ensued .

Now, without a belief system, and without prejudice, I have to verify anything that must sit inside my head. I am very much in touch with my ignorance. The things I do not know, I simply do not know.

One size does not fit all. I have learnt, through my life experience, that whatever I throw at life, life throws back at me. Therefore, I only do to others as I want them do to me. Do I want others to shield me when I do wrong? Not anymore. So I continually strive to do the right things the right way, in all things, and at all times.

A lot of people simply talk about things they have read in books and believe. But ask them to use their life experience to back up what they are saying and the experience contradicts beliefs. I know what works for me and what does not. To each his, or her own. A lot of Nigerians are expert when it comes to "God". But when it comes to their lives and the quality of life they live, the story is something else. Just look at Nigeria and Nigerians. Bribery and corruption galore is the order of the day! The weapon of corruption, weapon of poverty, seem to be prospering here in Nigeria. There ought to be a paradigm shift.

When I write anything that deals with issues of prayer and ethics, trust most Nigerians, they understand the prayer part- since that doesn't require great effort-and ignore the ethical/ moral part, which is so typical of an average hypocritical religious Nigerian religious person.

Good morals, high ethical standard, righteousness have taken the back seat while religious platitudes and unproductive religious rituals are the order of the day. It is no wonder that the country continues to descend into decadence, into chaos.

Majority of Nigerians are complaining. They are not satisfied with the way things are unfolding in their lives and in our country.

They say it themselves. They also say they are not fulfilled. It is obvious they have not found their "cheese".

I, of course, have found my "cheese'. I am fulfilled and I am content with life. Yet they think I ought to change my thinking to mirror their own. Their way of life is the only way, they think, with a faint but certain trace of delusional arrogance.

Hehehehehehe.

They are either comedians, or they misguided. The comprehension of reality has obviously eluded them. Frolicking in delusion, they keep searching for their own "cheese". They claim cheese but they are still "cheese-less".

Who moved their cheese? Please tell them quick. If the situation has changed, then, they ought to change. Or else.....

Have you found your "cheese"? I have found mine. And it is delicious. I find it in everyday living, in enjoying the simple pleasures of life, and not in perpetual hope of waiting for a brighter day. For me, every day is bright. I live. I love. I laugh. Every single day, no matter what. I have since gotten off the emotional roller coaster of life.

If you have found your "cheese", I rejoice with you. I can empathize with your inner bubbling. I can feel you, deeply.

If you have not, keep looking for it, realistically. And be humble, prudent enough to know that some never find "it" until they die.

I am an introvert and extrovert woven into one. I enjoy positive people's company. And I also enjoy my own company. I am a recluse, a bonafide hermit. While alone, enjoying the peace and joy of solitude, my thinking and I are best of friends. I control it and it controls me. But its control is limited to its conditioning.

This is true most of the time, but not all the time. Sometimes some thoughts that I did not think up myself will leap into my thought.

After analysis, or verification, if those thoughts are positive, beneficial, I let them stay inside my head. If not, I flush them down the drain. No one, no book controls my thoughts. But a silent voice in my abyss of thought is a constant guide. I am never bored, never sad. My thoughts and the silent voice are my constant companions. Their job is to keep me sane and sound. To keep me grounded in the objective reality that I share with you. To guide my behavior towards joy and peace and love. To make sure I always enjoy the simple pleasures of life. Ah! See why I do not import what I can produce. And why I do not search for what I have. I already have the kingdom of "God" within me.

I have never suffered in my life. Even during my "coldest winter ever" I did not suffer. PHCN tried, but I was not, and I am not perturbed. The frequent insufferable petrol scarcity too did not disturb my inner peace, my inner joy. The only thing that has the potential of making me to suffer is my mind, and the quality, accuracy of my thoughts. And over the years, I have tempered the power of my fiery soul. It is now gentle. And it allows me to live, love, and laugh.

Inner joy and inner peace have three fatal enemies: disappointment, frustration, and anger. Disappointment, frustration, and anger also have one fatal enemy: Accurate thinking/knowledge. In order to obtain inner peace and inner joy in this seemingly chaotic world, and, consequently attain emotional equilibrium, one has to acquire acuity, which is a prerequisite for acquiring accurate knowledge. Ignorance is no longer bliss!

Like I have written earlier, I discovered in 2000 that my praying or not praying had little effect on my experience, that consequences follow my right doings and wrong doings. Hence my decision to refrain from wrong doings and focus on right doings. I always reap what I sow, for me, is not a belief but an experience.

What is the purpose of life? Permit me to use my ignorance here: I do not know the purpose of life. However, I do know my purpose in life. Again, the discovery came seventeen years ago. What happens after death? You are asking the wrong man the right question. I simply do not know. I do not go beyond my experience; beyond what I can verify. My focus at this phase in my life is what is happening in Nigeria, the center of my world. Are we going to progress, regress, stagnate or disintegrate?

Do I "believe" I will ever eat amala again? Like I have said, I use beliefs sparingly. However, if I am still alive by this time tomorrow, it is more likely than not that I will eat amala and abula again.

In response to one of my Facebook posts, which naturally should have provoked thoughts, someone wrote:

"Don't forget there is Satan in the picture ruling the world presently..."

And I, in my uncharitable manner, responded:

"The Satan is in your mind, ruling your world, not mine. I have lived this long and I have never met this your imaginary Satan for once. Don't forget to think logically and critically when next you comment publicly."

I forgot to tell him that: "There is no space for Satan in my philosophical contraption. As a responsible adult, I am the one responsible for all my wrong doings"

I forgot to tell him that he needs a meditation class to help him cleanse and format his mind, to rid it of his childhood classical conditioning, so that he can have a mental picture of what reality is, and how it truly functions.

I have always said that ideals are good but practicality is what always matter to me. That is the core of my philosophy of life. If I cannot practicalize it, that idea may not be for me.

I am very cognizant of delusion that lurks in the mind. It tells people they could do what they are not capable of doing--false belief.

I am simply growing, within the confinement of my limitations. And perfection may not be within my scope.

But excellence is. Striving to do the right things the right way, in all things, and at all times, is pursuing excellence.

And just like Aristotle said, "We are what we repeatedly do. Excellence is not an accident but a habit."

CHAPTER 14

WE NEED A PARADIGM SHIFT

Mental models are deeply ingrained assumptions and generalizations that influence how we understand the world. Majority calls it beliefs. Until these are brought to the surface and thoroughly scrutinized, little knowledge takes place that does not conform to these models.

It should be obvious to any discerning soul that our mental models are not solving a lot of our problems. We need a paradigm shift. Where are the thinkers bold enough to challenge and critically analyze these mental models for their accuracy and conformance to our shared reality?

There are two concepts to choose from. One is "Abandonment to God" and the other is "Striving towards Perfection."

Admittedly there are situations where the "Abandonment to God" concept is applicable due to powerlessness, incubation, germination, evolution period.

However, life experience has taught me that I have been endowed, by "God", Universe, Allah or Evolution-depending on whatever the reader believes to be the Endowing Force--to have dominion over most things, albeit not all things. After all I could not remember deciding to be male, black, Nigerian.

Therefore, it is only natural to use my endowment by "Striving towards Perfection" which might be the deciding factor between success and failure. That is why striving to do the right things the right way has become my guiding principle.

Fortunately, both concepts accommodate "God". But, while proactive, hardworking, go-getting people might prefer "Striving towards Perfection", the reactive, lazy, clueless people may hide under "Abandonment to God".

At the end of the day, the difference in the choice we make will be clear for all to see. We will be able to tell the tree by the fruits it bears and not just by the promises it made.

Please I am not saying do not trust your "God", but always make sure you "tie your camel". Do not leave it untied and say "God" is in control", like our erstwhile President Goodluck Jonathan.

I was talking to someone sometimes in 2015, and she said that "God" will perfect everything about me. She thought she was praying for me. I asked her if it was "God's" job or my job to strive towards perfection by constant practice. In the customary fashion of the concept of "abandonment to God", she insisted it was God that will do it. Is it then not logical for people that think this way to be perpetually waiting on "God" to come and perfect our PHCN so we can have uninterrupted electric light? We need a paradigm shift in thinking if we want to move out of this quagmire we find ourselves.

We indeed need a Paradigm Shift. Because, the more we try to get "there" from "here", the more we could not, as a country, the more frustrated the majority of the citizens are becoming. And, we cannot get "there" from "here". Why? We have old "maps" that the majority cannot interpret correctly. Consequently, lasting success and enduring happiness continue to elude the majority.

One of the requirements of success and happiness is the ability to think clearly and accurately. One that does not think clearly and accurately cannot interpret "maps" correctly, cannot make effective decisions. And effective decisions are the foundation of lasting success and enduring happiness. We need to fine tune our decision-making skills. Because our decisions ultimately contribute largely to the quality of our lives

What is a Paradigm Shift? A paradigm shift is when a significant change happens, usually from one fundamental view to a different view. In most cases, some type of major discontinuity occurs as well. We majorly need a paradigm shift in our rigid cultural and religious beliefs.

It is important to note that beliefs initiate and guide actions. But beliefs can either guide actions in the right direction or in the wrong direction. "Suppose you want to arrive at a specific location in central Chicago, a street map of the city would be a great help to you in reaching your destination. But, suppose you were given the wrong map. Through a printing error, the map labelled 'Chicago' was actually a map for Detroit. Can you imagine

the frustration, the ineffectiveness of trying to reach your destination? You might work on your behavior---you could try harder, be more diligent, double your speed. But your efforts would only succeed in getting you to the wrong place faster. You might work on your attitude---you could think more positively. You still won't get to the right place, but perhaps you won't care. Your attitude would be so positive, but you'd still be lost. The fundamental problem has nothing to do with your behaviour or your attitude. It has everything to do with having the wrong map. If you have the right map of Chicago, then diligence becomes important, and when you encounter frustrating obstacles on the way, then attitude can make a real difference. But the first and most important requirement is the accuracy of the map.". 7 Habits of Highly Effective People by Stephen Covey.

The mental maps---mental models--- in our heads, where do they come from? Can we truthfully say, without fear of bearing false witness, that they have always, and will continuously take us to a desirable and favorable destination? As Nigerians, collectively, I will answer NO. That is why there must be a paradigm shift, there must be a rethink.

The seat of my soul has always been in Nigeria. Even when I was schooling, living abroad, this is where my heart has always been. This was where I was born, bred. And, hopefully, this is where I will die. Yes, Nigeria is ailing. Unprogressive minds populate her space. Corruption and incompetence are in abundant supply here. It is not just the artisans this applies to. Corruption and incompetence can be found at every level of Nigerian life. For most, it has become a culture, a way of life.

Yet, instead of most of our people to get on their feet, lace up their running shoes, to sprint towards progress, towards success and happiness, they usually go on their knees, to pray and ignore the required work of righteousness. They substitute religious rituals for upright living. But they ought to know that righteousness embedded in the culture of any country is what exalts it.

When I mention the word "religion", please always interpret it to mean all religions, both the imported ones and the local ones. None is immune to my constructive criticism.

Dissatisfaction is very pervasive here. This is a manifestation of spiritual/psychological malnourishment. In the midst of abundant water, a lot of people are still thirsty. Nigeria's President has his job cut out for him. I do not know how he will put new wine in old bottles.

The progress of this country is paramount to my soul. And I will keep saying my own until I die, or until we begin our journey in a favorable and desirable direction.

Barack Obama's election in the US was an American revolution, America's paradigm shift. For the son of an African immigrant man and a white American woman to rise to the topmost post in a country that was notorious for labelling anyone with a pinch of black blood black, and therefore a candidate for discrimination/ segregation, serious attitudinal change must had occurred to permit the paradigm shift/change.

We need this type of paradigm shift in Nigeria. No violence. Simple attitudinal change that will permit non-corrupt, competent, unbiased humans to rise and take their place in the circle of things. Our own paradigm shift/change must occur first before good things will descend on us. We need mental/cultural revolution in Nigeria. Start to work on your own mental/cultural revolution today. And let me work on mine. Together we can release ourselves from the shackles of backwardness. And consequently leap into the 21st century psychologically. It is all in our heads.

Sometimes in 2015, a friend and I needed to travel to Ilorin for her daughter's wedding. We needed a driver and someone sent us one. My friend asked the driver if he had a driver's license. And he said yes. She was satisfied with his answer. But I wasn't. I am into verification. Remember? So I demanded to see the license, while joking with him that I was a doubting Thomas. He searched through his wallet. But there was no license. He attempted to pass off his voter's card as a driver's license. He then claimed he must have forgotten it at home. The time was about 2pm. And we needed to get to Ilorin, from Lagos, that day. And I did not have a penchant for driving long distance. He drove. Hmmmm. A professional driver that was without his tool of trade.

Finally, during our ensuing conversation, I told him about corruption, about how it was not allowing us to grow and progress as a nation. But he could not see how his behavior contributed to the massive corruption pervading our country.

So I googled the word "corruption" for him. And the following was what I came up with: "Corruption is dishonest actions that destroys people's trust in the person or group, like the news of corruption in how your bank is run, that makes you close your account and invest your money somewhere else. The noun corruption comes from Latin — com ,or "with, together," and rumpere, meaning "to break." Corruption breaks your trustworthiness, your good reputation with others, like the news of corruption in the mayor's office that shocked everyone. When you corrupt something that is pure or honest, you take away those qualities. That's why "corruption of minors" is a serious offense in our legal system."

Corruption is "lack of integrity or honesty (especially susceptibility
 to bribery); use of a position of trust for dishonest gain.
"It is the inducement (as of a public official) by improper
means (as bribery) to violate duty (as by committing a felony)".

And it is the "decay of matter (as by rot or oxidation)"

I hope you can see why I have always insisted that majority of us are corrupt. It is true that a lot of us inherited these things called bribery and corruption. But we can use our brains by disinheriting them. They are debarring our growth and progress.

Few years ago, while on my evening stroll in my neighborhood, I ran into a woman arguing passionately with a man. Like a good Samaritan, I intervened. "What is the problem?"

The lady said she gave the man 500 Naira to buy petrol inside a five liter keg and the man came back with the keg not full. She went back to the petrol station to investigate and she found out that the man bought 400 Naira petrol and not 500 Naira. What could I say? The man had learned from bad leaders. Like leaders, like followers.

The following story also happened at a friend's pharmacy in Lagos. The cash register was not working in the pharmacy. No electricity to power it. The sales boy sold drugs worth of 4000 Naira, but recorded 3000 Naira in the sales register. And he pocketed the difference of 1000 Naira.

Thereafter, he complained about the ineptitude of PHCN and the massive corruption in our government, in our society, failing to see that he was a weak link in the chain of our national rebirth. Has it not been said that a chain is as strong as its weakest link?

When the sales-boy was caught stealing at the pharmacy he was suspended. Prior to the pocketing of the 1000 Naira, he had been warned for committing similar offense. At the disciplinary hearing, one person recommended termination and forfeiture of one month's pay. This, he said, would serve as punishment for the offender, as well as deterrence for the other staff members.

Another one begged on behalf of the offender, and asked for the offender to be given another chance. After all, as good Christians, they were supposed to forgive. Who had never sinned should cast the first stone, she said. The third person was swayed by the second person's appeal to religious/cultural sentiments. He opined that if the offender got fired, how was he going to be able provide daily bread for his family?

Like at the pharmacy, like in Nigeria. This happened in 2014. But it could easily have happened today.
'

I read the following quote somewhere: "Grace Is Not Just Leniency When We Sin, Grace Is God's Enabling Gift Not To Sin. Grace Is Power Not Just Pardon." I, of course, agree with it even though I am non-religious. This definition of grace makes a lot of sense to me. A saved soul ought to possess the power to shun vices, to resist evil, to shun corruption.

Nigeria needs a lot of saved souls that are rational, reasonable, and righteous, that possess the power to shun corruption, to resist evil, to live exemplary upright lifestyles. We definitely need a paradigm shift. Economic power can be taken away, but no one can take away the reasoning ability of another.

Bows and arrows and spears have been overpowered by guns and bombs and drones. The world has evolved and moved on. We need to wake up and start moving. The most important place to start is inside our minds. Primitive minds cannot produce a modern world.

"We cannot solve our problems with the same thinking we used when we created them", said Albert Einstein. Our refusal, or inability, to think critically, logically, creatively is responsible for a lot of the challenges we have today individually and collectively. And until we rebel/revolt intellectually, creatively, nothing much is going to change. "Change will not come if we wait for some other person or some other time. We are the ones we've been waiting for. We are the change that we seek" Barack Obama

No one can plant beans and expect to harvest rice. No one. Instead of us looking inward and looking in the mirror to make the necessary changes that will order our lives and our nation, majority of us are busy waiting for miracles, waiting for manna to drop from the sky. We fail to realize that we are the change we are waiting for, a la Obama. We are the ones that must align our thinking and behaviors to correspond with the consequences we so desire. Think of a car. And think of wheel alignment. If the wheels are not in alignment, the car will wobble. And that sweet, smooth ride will be disturbed.

No one, I repeat, no one can plant beans and expect to harvest rice. If it is not favorable, even if desirable, get rid of it. Move into

the 21st century by producing favorable thoughts. Unshackle
your mind from archaic thoughts, even if desirable. Drug users
find getting high desirable even though it is not favorable on the
long run. Allow the change to begin with you.

CHAPTER 15

WE REAP WHAT WE SOW

We've prayed.
We've hoped.
We've fasted.
We've paid our tithes.
And we've even spent sleepless nights at night vigil.
The only thing missing is, "treat people the way we want to be treated."

Treating others the way we want to be treated is fairness. It is doing the right things the right way.

The core of the message of all religions is: Do unto others as you want done unto you. If we all abide by this principle as the essence of "God", we will not go wrong.

"The law of harvest is to reap more than you sowed. Sow an act and you reap a habit. Sow a habit and you reap a character. Sow a character and you reap a destiny." - Unknown.

Just imagine the following story:

He was executing a government contract in Ijebu Igbo in Ogun State and he decided to go and inspect the project one day.

He left from Lagos early in the morning. He stopped somewhere on the Lagos-Ibadan Expressway to buy cold drinks. He was about to drive off when a thought came to his mind. "Buy bags of pure water for the workers." He got down from the car and bought the bags of pure water, then, onward to Ijebu Igbo he proceeded.

He was about to exit at Sagamu when his car engine cut off. He pulled to the side of the road to check what happened. Alas, steam was coming from the car engine! The car had overheated without the car indicator alerting him!

Okay, he had experienced overheating before so he knew what to do: wait till the car cooled off and add water inside the radiator. Where would he get water from in the middle of nowhere?

Then he remembered the bags of pure water he bought earlier for the construction workers and he smiled, happy that he had honoured the "thought" that came to his mind earlier.
The car cooled off, and he poured the water inside the radiator, then, onward he continued his journey to Ijebu Igbo, for daily bread.

That man was me. And that experience further reinforced the concept that "I always reap what I sow, good or bad, big or small."

This is what I told someone: I don't pray anymore. I stopped in 2000, about seventeen years ago after I realized that it was not working for me. I also discovered that I mostly reap what I sowed. I was able to link most of my challenges, my problems, to my prior incorrect decisions, ineffective, or downright wrong actions.

Consequently, I began to think, to plan to achieve anything I want within the scope of my human and financial resources. I began to only do those things that would ultimately lead to the satisfaction of my needs and wants. However, I pruned unnecessary wants from my psyche. I collapsed my belief system and replaced it with "conscious ignorance".

Aha! Cognitive dissonance disappeared. Delusion dissipated. Unrealistic hope/expectations vanished. Disappointment, gone.

Frustration, dead. Happiness, joy bloomed. Love gushed. Peace erupted. Contentment carpeted my entire being. No more hatred. No space for malice and bitterness. I could peacefully, easily disengage from relationships that had gone sour due to irreconcilable differences.

That was when I began to live, love, and laugh. That was how I got to become who I am today.

And someone said, but you must pray ceaselessly. Prayer is the master key. Don't you believe in God? Ehen, you could not do anything on your own o. How can you get unmerited favor if you don't pray?
I think the person asking me the question is spiritually blind.
He does not know what the fruits look, taste like.

That was when it dawned on me that I was actually trying to do the impossible: have a discussion with a book, and not a conscious human being that was conscious of his ignorance. The urge to point out to him all his inadequacies that his ceaseless prayer, his master key left in my full glare dissipated.

Of course I knew he would have retaliated by lecturing me about his imaginative heaven, hell, salvation, rapture, eternity, etc. Of course I was aware that he was an expert on what and who "God" is, His wants and needs, even His favorite dishes. And I was also aware that he had no clue on how to translate all that knowledge into living a peaceful, joyous and fulfilling life. The concept of sowing and reaping means little to him. Of course I pity him. Only if...

A lot of us want what we did not work for. We want what we do not deserve. We want to reap where we did not sow. We fail to realize that those who reap without sowing may later sow without reaping.

Some people said I am only saying this because I do not understand what unmerited favor is. How productive, progressive will a country where the majority get what they did not work for, what they do not deserve? Corruption and incompetence will be in abundant supply in that country. There' is no substitute for doing the right things the right way, if not in all things, in most things, if not at all times, at least most of the time. And it must be without hypocrisy. Most of the time, we always reap what we sowed, good or bad, big or small.

Maybe our current recession and weakening Naira are the result of unmerited favor? If it is not so sad, so painful, it would have been funny. Some of the by-products of uprightness, apart from the fact that it keeps a country vibrant, are enduring happiness and lasting success for a large section of the citizenry.

Doing the same things we have always done will only result in getting the same things we've always gotten. Always remember that anything left by itself will go from bad to worse if nothing is done to prevent that.

Look at our country, the recession, and our ever-weakening Naira. Is "God" no longer in control as our so-called religious, political leaders are wont to be telling us? Why are things going from bad to worse? Is it because people do not pray or pay tithes?

"If you want to change your life, first you must change your thoughts." But, how can folks who never created their own thoughts know how to change thoughts? I think it is unintelligent to think we can pray our way out of situations we behaved ourselves into. "God" is not deaf. "God" is not blind.

I spoke to Status Quo in the last day of 2016, as I always do every day. As usual, we debated. We argued, sometimes with loud voices, but with humility, with respect.

Again, both of us did not yield. We did not shift position. I wanted the present situation to change. And Status Quo wanted the present situation to remain. He said what was my own wahala, that almost everyone in Nigeria loved him, with their thinking, with their beliefs, and with their behavior.

I told him to have a rethink, that a determined minority is emerging. And it is full of disdain for Status Quo. Status Quo panicked. For the first time, he seemed to be in doubt of the undying love the majority has for him and his malicious hold on the lives of millions.

As he customarily did, Status Quo did not win the debate. He did not win the argument. Yes, this was a democracy, designed for the majority to win. But the majority's camp was in disarray, no longer sure of what the future held.

With no trophy in his hand, and no glee in his eyes, the majority, instead of carrying Status Quo shoulder high, savoring the sweetness of victory, scampered into their respective homes, with uncertainty, the first in many years.

I, on the other hand, politely retreated from the contest arena. I retreated to my peaceful haven, to sharpen my "saw", to strategise about Change, convinced as ever that, as an initial matter, change must occur first, if this country was to move forward, to progress.

While in solitude, I looked in my hand. And the inner joy, inner peace, the sense of a life that was ordered that I carry everywhere I go. And I thought these were enough reward for me even if the country with a displeased majority refused to change.

Ki a gun Iyan si inu ewe. Ki a se obe si inu epo epa. Eni ma yo a yo. Let us pound yam inside a leaf, put soup inside a groundnut shell, those who will be satisfied will be satisfied. So is my case with Nigeria. I will continue to live, love, and laugh, regardless of what the majority decides to do. To each his/her own. I am getting mine, not by mere wishing/praying. But by striving to do the right things the right way, sans corruption. I hope you get yours.

And every year, I want to interact with only those who can "learn", "see", and "do". Life is too short to continue to deal with those that are comfortable with stagnation. I am neither a pastor nor a politician. So, quality must trump quantity every new year. The quality of people I deal with is going to ultimately determine the quality of my connection power. After all, I always reap what I sow

CONCLUSION

Resilience is defined as "the ability to become strong, healthy, or successful again after something bad happens" It is also "the ability of something to return to its original shape after it has been pulled, stretched, pressed, bent, etc."

If Nigerians are to be called "resilient", what original shape will they return to after all the pulling down, stretching out, and pressing we've been through? Is it before the infiltration of Islam and Christianity? Or is it colonization? Put another way, what is the original shape of the average Nigerian? Does the average Nigerian either know, or care? Yet, he must not only know, but he must also care. Because it is a national tragedy to think an externally imposed shape is one's original shape. And a consequence of that is the loss of the "the ability to become strong, healthy, or successful again after something bad happens.

"When you squeeze an orange, orange juice comes out — because that's what's inside. When you are squeezed, what comes out is what is inside." - Dr. Wayne Dyer

We are now being squeezed. It is time to let what's inside to come out. The real you that has been submerged by what was originally outside that was rammed into us through conquest, through colonization, with the aids of classical conditioning and learned helplessness.

It is simply time to think, and rethink, time to arrange, and rearrange thoughts. I have started my own journey few years back.

Refrain from parroting what others have said or written. Look into your mind, at what you observe, at your life experiences, and make statements you can verify within the context of your life.

Since the individual is the building blocks of any society, the individual is the starting point of the Nigerian reformation. The best place to commence the cleaning of this society is within the individual soul. The best time to start is now. Curb corruption. Unblock and enlighten your mind. Become less profligate. Improve your competence. Be fair to your fellow human beings. The individuals make up society. The society makes up the government. Without this cleaning, waiting for election time to pick "better" candidate is simple, if not complex delusion. Is democracy not the government of the people by the people for the people?

I have always maintained that prayer is an exercise in futility if not coupled with "doing the right things the right way, in all things, and at all times."

So, to those who think I am wrong, that they can achieve what their hands do not work for, by simply enlisting the power of prayer, how did we arrive at this junction where the Naira is at its weakest and the prices of essential commodities have since doubled, in spite of our collective prayer?

How? How? How?

Prayer is not the solution to our national ailments. Neither is fasting. Forget tithes paying too. There is nothing holy in it. It is simply the payment one pays for importing the brand of thinking one cannot produce.

Having effective religious, political, traditional leaders who inspire, compel us to do the right things, the right way, in all things, and at all times is the solution.

No one can plant corn and reap beans. No amount of praying and fasting can achieve that. "God" is not deaf.

EPILOGUE

In 1997, five of us got together to brainstorm about Africa. Why was Africa lagging behind the rest of the word in terms of technological growth? During our brainstorming sessions, we all realized the need for us to have a common vision that could guide our actions.

Even though we all share the same African ancestry, we were not from the same country. One was from Haiti. Another one was from Belize. I was from Nigeria. And, the remaining two were from Jamaica and USA respectively.

We recognized that our ideology was foreign to us. Even though I was the only one from the African continent, my own ideology was foreign too. Imagine that. I could not even provide them with a home-grown effective ideology.

We all agreed that crafting a wholesale ideology that we all could embrace was absolutely necessary.

But before we would proceed with the formulation of ideology, we recognized the need to define our own individual reality first. And that was how D.O.O.R was born.

The full meaning of D.O.O.R. is Defining Our Own Reality. D.O.O.R is for independent and creative thinkers who are capable of defining their own reality instead of allowing others to define their reality for them.

And these are the prerequisite steps in Defining Our Own Reality.

Discover who you are.

Discover your talents.

Acquire the necessary knowledge to develop your talents.

Develop the pertinent skills to utilize your talents and knowledge.

Know what you want out of life. And focus on it.

Know how to use your talents, knowledge and skills to get what you want out of life.

Gain the mastery of success and happiness.

Put your talents, knowledge, and skills to better yourself, your family, your country.

Hopefully, with more people recognizing the need to accept responsibility for their lives, and taking the initiative to self-develop themselves, we will begin to climb the ladder of success. And, ultimately, our status of being Third World Countries will change.

9 789789 588190